"This is an engaging story about t[...] wou[...] [...]and even from the church—that can be [...]sed to [...]

—M. CRAIG BARNES
Princeton Theological Seminary

"David Howell is a great storyteller, and his story will intersect in one way or another with every reader I can imagine."

—BRIAN MCLAREN
Author of *We Make the Road by Walking*

"I love it! . . . such a fine way of storytelling . . ."

—THOMAS G. LONG
Candler School of Theology

". . . clear, persuasive, and so well written . . ."

—WALTER BRUEGGEMANN
Columbia Seminary

". . . a lovely, readable style . . ."

—BARBARA BROWN TAYLOR
New York Times bestselling author

"I am greatly enjoying 'poop in the boots,' 'all about the Murdocks,' 'Elvis at the Nu Wray Inn.'"

—DONALD DAVIS
Featured Storyteller, National Storytelling Festival

"Christian preaching is the act of proclaiming how the story of Jesus Christ rewrites our own stories. David Howell's memoir narrates just how it is that God makes a preacher."

—ROLF JACOBSON
Author of *Crazy Talk: A Not-So-Stuffy Dictionary of Theological Terms*

"Sitting upon the porch of David Howell's imagination we are given the gift of listening to a Southern storyteller, preacher, prophet, and stirrer of holy mischief. This spiritual memoir offers the reader a window into rugged, pragmatic, and complex theological thought peppered with a heavy dose of compassion."

—OTIS MOSS III
Senior Pastor, Trinity United Church of Christ, Chicago

"This remarkable book seems to provide evidence that once the world was denser with stories. Funny ones, scary ones, poignant ones—an accumulation of stories that make a life and a community."

—BILL MCKIBBEN
Author of *Wandering Home*

"David Howell's telling of his coming of age in the provincial Appalachian town of Boonford, North Carolina enthralled me from the start. From a gasp of horror to an all-out belly laugh, it brought a much-needed lightning flash of delight to my reading queue. *Tethered to an Appalachian Curse* delivers story after amazing story of hilarity, tragedy, sex, lyin' and cheatin', drunkenness, heartbreak, and grace-filled redemption of Old Testament proportions as they unfold among the citizens of this tiny North Carolina town. In his whimsical, down-to-earth way, Howell reminds us of our own journeys to find purpose, and our life-long attempts to prove we belong in the very arms of love that have claimed us all along."

—PETER MAYER
Lead Vocalist and Guitarist, the Peter Mayer Group

"David Howell possesses the two indispensable ingredients of all gifted writers. He is a consummate storyteller, and he has an incredible story to tell. Across the pages of this book, the grace of God is neither an abstract concept nor a pious sentiment, but rather it shows up in the nitty-gritty and sometimes painful details of our lives to guide, encourage, and ennoble. You will be drawn into Howell's superbly written and breathtakingly honest story from the very first page, and you will be blessed by reading it."

—DAVID J. LOSE
Author of *Preaching at the Crossroads*

"Howell's tales will engage you, amuse you, provoke you, and keep you turning the pages to read more. For all those blessed with an open mind, who refuse to settle for false platitudes and condemnations, who hunger for real substance . . . there is much here to feast upon."

—MICHAEL B. CURRY
Author of *Love is the Way*

"What a tale David Howell has to tell, and how well he tells it. Rarely has the plight of poor, Southern mountain people been told so well (or so honestly). Almost never have we had a more inspiring story of a person's journey from dire, difficult childhood into ministerial service. The creator of the wildly successful Festival of Homiletics gives us a front-row seat whereby we can see the tug of God on a life, the adventure and mystery of Christian vocation."

—WILL WILLIMON
Duke Divinity School

"Sometimes we think of our vocational paths in terms of straight lines: a single course that is ours to discern, set, and follow in one direction. But David Howell reminds us that vocation can also be a journey of discovery with many joyful twists and turns if we let the forks in the road and unexpected side trips lead us into new adventures—not just once, but again and again! Howell's stories of what he has seen and learned along the way will inspire you to take a few more leaps of faith yourself. Here is a book to encourage, embolden, and enjoy."

—ANNA CARTER FLORENCE
Columbia Seminary

"Life stories can be dull, or predictable, or pedestrian. Not David Howell's. A rollicking ride through unfamiliar turf that reveals something at the core of every one of us. Highly recommended!"

—JAMES HOWELL
Senior Pastor, Myers Park United Methodist Church

"I was tethered to David Howell's memoir of childhood, sin, redemption, revelation, and honest searching from the first page. His loving and compassionate portrayal of his rearing is a powerful antidote to the usual pap about rural Appalachian life. A longtime resident and lover of small-town Southern life, I laughed, cried, nodded, and reveled in the intimate telling of his evolution from a hellfire-and-brimstone preacher's curse to a wise and inspiring purveyor of open-hearted Christianity. And it goes without saying that my mouth watered repeatedly at the glorious description of wonderful food. Cornbread smoothie? Indeed! The whole book is like a good bowl of soup beans . . . nutritious and satisfying."

—JOHN MCCUTCHEON
Singer, Songwriter, Storyteller

"I really, really enjoyed David's memoir. As I read the book, the voice of a storyteller emerged. I could hear his words as they moved into images, and then the characters, communities, and worlds were conjured—what a ride . . . it is a true gift. Even a flatlander from the North can identify with David's people. I know these folks, those succeeding despite themselves—a world where profound beauty is often wrapped in desperate times, humor arrives at the most unlikely moment, and to be human is on full display. Like all good guides, David is on the journey with us and proves time and again that people everywhere love, hate, and desire as much as any king or queen that ever lived."

—KEVIN KLING
Storyteller

"I am a city girl through and through, raised in a vibrant postwar Philadelphia neighborhood of row houses, concrete sidewalks, and asphalt streets. But from David's opening description of 'Reverend Leroy,' the 'Born Again Church,' the miners, and the 'baccer' farmers of the Appalachian community of his childhood, I settled with ease into the front-porch view his writing offers the reader. This wonderfully written memoir is a touchstone, a journey through and reminder of the multilayered complexities of immigrant origins, family history, community beliefs and dynamics, and the distinctive, colorful inhabitants and interrelationships that shape our identities and the paths we choose to take. This book, with David's effective storytelling style, is recommended reading for anyone who may be giving thought to writing their own memoir."

—**CHARLOTTE BLAKE ALSTON**
Storyteller, Narrator, Librettist

"David Howell writes about growing up in a region in Appalachia buried in poverty, infected with racism, and terrorized by a local preacher who is certain that David is destined to end up in hell. Through a combination of divine interventions and perseverance, he moves from the hills of Appalachia to the halls of Union Theological Seminary in New York City and beyond, eventually establishing the Festival of Homiletics. This is a story of God's amazing grace!"

—**MARVIN A. MCMICKLE**
Ashland Theological Seminary

"More than being tethered to an Appalachian curse, David Howell's life story reveals how he's been tethered to the Spirit of surprise callings. The details of his journey may be particular, but what is universal is the underlying hopeful message that an unsolicited curse can become an unforeseen blessing."

—**LUKE A. POWERY**
Duke Divinity School

Tethered to an Appalachian Curse

Tethered to an Appalachian Curse

A Surprise Calling

David Brown Howell

RESOURCE *Publications* · Eugene, Oregon

TETHERED TO AN APPALACHIAN CURSE
A Surprise Calling

Resource Publications
An Imprint of Wipf and Stock Publishers
199 W. 8th Ave., Suite 3
Eugene, OR 97401

www.wipfandstock.com

PAPERBACK ISBN: 978-1-6667-0396-2
HARDCOVER ISBN: 978-1-6667-0397-9
EBOOK ISBN: 978-1-6667-0398-6

07/12/21

Note: Fictitious names are used in this autobiographical novel, except for immediate family members and professional colleagues.

For my parents, Lena and Jack
For siblings, Larry and Carolyn
For cousin, Dennis
For children, Wendy, Shannon, Meredith, Morgan
For grandchildren, Zina, Aidan, Reese, Nolan, Maddox, Abby
For great granddaughter, Capri
For Mary, Nathan, and Jake
For my favorite theologian, Mary Ann Howell

Contents

Salvation's Slippery Slope

"There was never an uninteresting life.
Such a thing is an impossibility.
Inside the dullest exterior there is a drama,
a comedy, and a tragedy."
—MARK TWAIN

"The business of life is the acquisition of memories."
—MR. CARSON, HEAD BUTLER, *DOWNTON ABBEY*

THUNDER RATTLES THE SKY. Evening storm clouds race away over the mountain peaks. Sun shines brightly for a few moments and slips beneath the earth. A flock of blackbirds flutters into the dusk. The storm leaves the sweet smell of summer rain filling the air.

Several men stand outside Born Again Church, a building with old, white clapboard siding, rust-speckled tin roof, and sacred windows depicting the life of Jesus like many small churches scattered across the Appalachian Mountains. On one side of the church flows a small sparkling creek with empty pork and beans cans and bottles washed down its edges. On the other side, a caramel brown, clay bank, with no vegetation, towers over the church building.

The men outside the church know what's in store for them inside. As a distraction, they talk quietly about the upcoming hunting season for they know the fiery preacher's words will deeply unsettle them. Eddie Crawford last attended church on Easter Sunday, months ago. He wears the same dress clothes today: baggy black pants, cowboy emblem belt,

1

and white shirt with embroidered pockets. He stiffens and says to the others: "You boys ready for this? That preacher goin' make believers out of us yet! We're goin' to Hell if we don't get saved!" Toby Greene shakes his head in begrudging submission, wishing he could have flown away with the flock of blackbirds. Waiting until the last minute to enter the sanctuary, feet squirm side to side mashing out cigarette butts on the ground. Already inside the church, women mill around and chatter quietly among themselves, then start finding their seats.

Already seated, Jack Howell, a rugged miner with wavy brown hair and blue eyes, uncomfortable in dress slacks and white shirt, stares out the open church window at a large mackerel tabby cat toying with a gray mouse. He sits nervously on the well-worn, rickety back pew on this warm August evening in 1951. Jack's gaze switches back and forth from the cat's deadly game to the pulpit where the flamboyant preacher in a raspy baritone begins to bellow out eternal condemnations on sinners. Full of rhetorical adrenaline, his message sizzles on the brains of the un-educated farmers, miners, and mill workers in the pews.

Jack's wife, Lena, with her auburn hair and green eyes, is skinny thin from a life of poverty and poor nutrition. Keenly interested in what the preacher says, Lena worries she's not "saved." The intense preacher with a full head of thick, greased, combed-back dark hair, and bushy, imposing, eyebrows proclaims convincingly the "unsaved" will roast in the fires of Hell. With salacious details, the golden-throated preacher describes eternal agony in the flames. Extinction is preferable to Hell but not an option, he warns them. Will Lena get saved? What about Jack?

Born Again Church buzzes with life as the center of the community in Boonford, North Carolina. The explorer Daniel Boone fords the roaring North Toe River here, and leaves behind a few relatives, my ancestors. Folks here are miners, "baccer" (tobacco) farmers, and mill "hands." It is a community where you are either a member of the church or else you are a sinner and a reprobate in the eyes of church members and the pastor, Reverend Leroy. The Reverend is neither seminary educated nor does he want to be. Seminaries are not only liberal, but most are agents of the Devil himself.

Reverend Leroy escapes a tough life in Transylvania County, North Carolina. After high school, Leroy hitchhikes to Burnsville and secures a job working the graveyard shift at Glen Hill Hosiery Mill. Five years later, falling asleep at the wheel on the way home, he swerves into the other lane striking a small car carrying two women on their way to their jobs as cooks in the cafeteria of Cane River High School. One woman died on the scene and the other a few days later in the hospital. Leroy slipped into a deep depression, "took to the bottle," and lost his job.

Two years after the accident, Leroy walks into the Sunday morning service at Born Again Church, noticed by all the fine folks in church since Leroy never set foot in a church before. Aging Pastor Jones gives a slow, plodding sermon on the Apostle Paul's conversion on the Damascus Road. Pastor Jones issues the obligatory altar call after his sermon. Not a single soul has responded to the Pastor's altar calls recently, only Maybelle Fortner after she got her cancer diagnosis more than a year ago. But this morning the call from the altar does not go unheeded. Leroy confidently strolls forward putting his arm around feeble Pastor Jones. Standing nostril to nostril with Pastor Jones, Leroy says he is ready to confess his sins and give his life to the Lord. He is on his knees before Pastor Jones can invite him to kneel. Leroy prays one of the most eloquent prayers Boonford has ever heard. Jaws drop in the congregation. Husbands and wives turn to look at each other in amazement. A little boy whispers to his mother, "Mama, where did he come from?"

Six months later, Pastor Jones dies of an apparent heart attack on Christmas Day. Newly appointed Sunday School teacher Leroy has a packed house every Sunday morning during the Sunday School hour. Arrive early for Leroy's class for a seat or stand around the walls as many do. Pastor Jones's widow asks Leroy to lead the service for her beloved husband's funeral. Leroy graciously accepts, preaches "as fine a sermon as we've ever heard" and leaves people saying "Leroy should be a preacher!"

The Board of Deacons meets the next evening, decides the funeral sermon was Leroy's trial sermon, and enthusiastically issue him a unanimous invitation to be their next pastor. Like many mountain preachers, Leroy does not study for the ministry. He experiences "a calling from the Lord" and abruptly switches careers overnight, from a drunk to a hellfire and brimstone preacher. He is now Pastor Leroy. Some say so persuasive and charismatic, he could sell sand to a man dying of thirst.

Lena and Jack Howell aren't members of Born Again Church, nor do they attend any church. But there are lots of new faces this summer evening in Born Again Church. Reverend Leroy's golden tongue reputation spreads like wind-driven wildfire. Normally the church invites a guest preacher to preach the annual August revival series (Monday through Thursday), but church members are so enthralled with their new pastor's electrifying sermons they vote for Leroy to preach every evening of the revival. Church members whisper rumors he does not have to prepare his sermons. He simply prays, and the words come to him.

Lena's friends insist she attend the Monday evening service. Jack suffering from a life-long social anxiety disorder has no interest in attending, but he talks about buying a new twenty-two caliber rifle. Buying a rifle is a big deal financially. They are so poor at this time that they cut each other's hair and pull each other's teeth when needed. But Lena really wants to go to the revival. A deal is struck . . . go to church and Jack can buy the gun.

Jack's family (Howell) already condemned to Hell by the pastor, so his attendance is doubly interesting. One of the Howells is a functional polygamist with two common-law wives, one in Boonford and one in South Carolina ("down off the mountain"). He simply splits his time between the families as he hauls produce (cabbage and beans "produced" in the mountains) to Spartanburg and returns with peaches and watermelons grown in warmer climates in the south. From the pulpit, Pastor Leroy in a scorching sermon pronounces damnation upon the polygamist.

Bud, Jack's uncle, lives beside the church parsonage, the home provided for the pastor. The uncle is a farmer, growing the cabbage and beans hauled and sold by his brother in South Carolina. So it happens one Saturday afternoon while Pastor Leroy prepares his sermon that my great uncle Bud Howell plows his field.

Bud uses a cultivating plow between rows of cabbage to turn the weeds under the soil. This is far easier than chopping weeds with a hoe. Plowing in the mountains is still done mostly by mules in the early 1950s. Folks are poor and cannot afford tractors. Plowing with a mule takes a special vocabulary. A well-trained mule knows to stay between the rows and not walk on the vegetable rows. As the mule approaches the end of the row, the educated mule waits for a one-word cue from the farmer behind the plow. "Gee" means to turn right, and "Haw" means to turn left. If the mule goes the wrong way, there are all kinds of possible problems, like damaging part of the row of vegetables or simply wasting time going the wrong way and having to turn around. There are times when either Bud or the mule are apparently dyslexic. Bud wants the mule to turn left and shouts out "Haw," but the mule goes right. Or maybe Bud wants to go left and mistakenly says "Gee." Whatever the reason, when that happens and the mule goes in the wrong direction, Bud unleashes a firestorm of profanity, and he has a rich vulgar vocabulary. Bud does not want his mule to be "stubborn as a mule."

Across the field, Pastor Leroy prepares his sermon at the kitchen table. In the mountains, these are days still without air-conditioning. It is summer with windows open. Whenever Bud's old mule turns the wrong way, colorful profanity streams through the windows to the preacher's ears like a strong gust from the disgusting bowels of Hades. After a Saturday of plowing, cursing, and frustrated sermon writing, Pastor Leroy in the Sunday morning service with a voice slashing like a sword declares from all he has seen and heard that all the Howells are going to Hell.

With good reason to be nervous, Jack sits on that shaky old back pew in the Born Again Church. Like all the Howells, already condemned to Hell, his tormented fate awaits him in the after-life. On the other hand, Lena, not a "blood" Howell, wonders if there might be some eternal hope for her? As her heart hammers in her chest, Lena wonders if maybe she goes forward as they sing "Amazing Grace" she will escape the unending torture and torment described so vividly by Pastor Leroy. Five people walk the aisle to the altar during the singing of the hymn.

Pastor Leroy roars, "Five people came forward. They will escape the blistering, flesh-burning fires of Hell, but there're others out there, and you know who you are! You're on a slippery slope straight through the wide-open gates of Satan's Hell! We'll sing 'Amazing Grace' one last time. It might be your final chance to be saved, to spend eternity with the righteous where there is no pain, no suffering, no more death. The unrighteous will spend their every second in eternal agony! Do you want that? You want your families someday seeing you roasting in Hell? Won't you come while we sing?"

As the congregation sings, the unexpected happens. Two women sitting about halfway back rise up and head toward the rear pew where a nervous Jack and a hyperventilating Lena, a mass of terror swelling up in her stomach, are seated. Lena happens to be closest to the aisle. The first woman, a gnarled strong mill worker with skin from hard work as tough as old leather, grabs Lena's left arm and pulls her into the aisle. The other surly built woman with a face like a puckered prune takes the right arm. They pull Lena up toward the altar where a smiling Pastor Leroy waits with open arms. The gnarled woman says to Lena, "We want you to go to Heaven with us. We're taking you to the Lord!"

Lena wants to get saved, but part of her wants to stay with Jack . . . it doesn't feel right to leave him alone in the pew. Jack spent his adult life in the mines, dodging falling rocks and near disasters. So he learned to respond quickly. Jack jumps to his feet, takes huge strides down the aisle, and wrestles Lena away from her would-be angelic rescuers. Out the door they flee, never to set foot again in Born Again Church, as Pastor Leroy boasts loudly to his congregation, "See I told you, all the Howells are going to Hell! They turned their backs on the altar of salvation!"

Lena is eight months pregnant this warm August evening in the little church on top of the mountain. I am in her womb. And as my uncle, who told me this story, says, "Dave, you almost got saved that night! You almost got to the altar."

"David, you have lived a charmed life." *New York Times* bestselling author Barbara Brown Taylor says to me at a conference in 2015 after I share my plan to semi-retire. I have not shared my story with Barbara. She doesn't know about my close call with salvation on that warm evening in 1951. She doesn't know about my growing up poor as dirt in the Appalachian Mountains or my desperate search for acceptance. Nor does she know about my life-long struggle, like my father, with a social anxiety disorder. I earned seminary degrees and enjoyed a life crisscrossing the globe. I spoke in the National Cathedral in Washington DC. I've been in the company of Nobel Peace Prize winners, Pulitzer Prize winners, U.S. Senators, Civil Rights activists, famed musicians, U.S. Poet Laureates, and for all I know still might not be saved? Can the Howells escape the curse of damnation from Reverend Leroy? Will I ever find salvation? Does it even matter?

So this is the story of a womb dweller who barely misses out on salvation before birth and of a theologically confused young man who struggles to find acceptance and meaning in a world while tethered to a curse of eternal damnation.

Ole' Daniel Boone and River of Death

"We can complain because rose bushes have thorns
or rejoice because thorn bushes have roses . . ."
—ABRAHAM LINCOLN

BOONFORD WELCOMED ME INTO the world, warmly nurtured me, and terrified me. Not on any map, truly a time-forgotten little place laced with roaring rivers and railroad tracks. Boonford, settled by both sets of my ancestors (Boones and Howells), bustles with activity in its time. In the late 1800s and early 1900s Boonford has a railroad depot and a country store, owned by an ancestor, Charlie Howell who always had part of his breakfast in his beard. When the railroad decides to carry only coal and no passengers, the depot closes. But Charlie Howell's store continues to be the center of community life until the automobile gives people more mobility. The train does not stop anymore but slows down enough for a railroad employee clinging from the side to hang a bag of mail on a track-side pole. Charlie and his wife Lizzie, a humorous sight as she always wear "galoshes" and denim overalls, then put the mail in individual boxes in the store.

Bound for the cities of the east coast, coal trains from Kentucky wind their way out of Tennessee and up through the Nolichucky Gorge and through Boonford. The gorge is a filming location for *The Last of the Mohicans* starring Daniel Day-Lewis. The Mohican tribe lived in upstate New York, but the movie director preferred the rugged mountains of North Carolina. Nolichucky is from a Cherokee word meaning "river of death." The rushing waters of the Nolichucky claim the lives of many over the years. A train left its tracks and fell into the river. A sunken railcar

7

remains in the river near the entrance to the famed "Lost Cove," an abandoned settlement accessible only by foot-trail. Hikers to this day enjoy trekking the trail into "Lost Cove" where legendary size snakes have been spotted in the old houses.

The residents of Boonford buried their dead in a small cemetery next to the railroad tracks. Graves were covered with stones, and wooden markers revealed the names of those in the ground. The officials of Clinchfield Railroad in the early 1900s inform the residents of Boonford they have to move their dead, saying they were too close to the tracks. The residents considered that to be the ultimate insult and refused for years to move the graves. Finally, they relented and moved the graves to the new Boonford Cemetery, located between Sqally and Wing (they had great names for their communities).

As they often do, the teenagers of Boonford deal sweet revenge on Clinchfield. One night they hunker in the now-empty graves after painting their faces with white paint. When the night train approaches, they raise up out of "their graves" and put a temporary fright into the conductor and crew. On another occasion, the boys fill sacks with cow manure and add a splash of kerosene. They set fire to the sacks as the train rounds the bend. The conductor applies the brakes and brings the train to a hissing stop. The conductor and several rail-hands jump off the train and stomp the bags. A sweet, smelly revenge accomplished!

The origins of Boonford go back to Wales and England. Squire Boone, Sr., a Quaker fleeing persecution, emigrates from England in the early 1700s and settles outside present-day Philadelphia. His sons Daniel Boone and Israel Boone migrate down the Shenandoah Valley into the mountains of North Carolina. Israel and his wife die, leaving two children. Daniel and Rebecca raise my great, great, great, great grandfather, Jonathan Boone. Daniel and the young Jonathan are the first explorers of the area. Reaching the North Toe River, today the boundary between Yancey and Mitchell counties, they ford the river. In a few years as other settlers reach the area it is dubbed Boonford (probably "Boones' Ford" originally), "cause Ole Daniel crossed here."

Jonathan Boone's grandson and Daniel's great-nephew, Robert Boone, fights in the Mexican War (1846) and the Civil War (1861). Captured by the northern army at Gettysburg, Robert spends the remainder of the war in a Union prison camp. When my uncle John Boone died owning Robert Boone's toolbox, the family decided that I should have the toolbox which I have in safe-keeping to this day. Family lore contends that the toolbox made it into the Mexican War and into the Civil War. Apparently, Robert Boone was an artillery mechanic and kept his tools in the wooden box.

The Howells date their ancestry back to Hwyel the Good, King of Wales (880–948). He was proclaimed the Good because of a system of just and fair laws he instituted for his citizens, and he also kept France's William the Conqueror out of Wales. However, by the 1600s, conditions in many parts of Europe were unbearable for common people. In the 1700s, William Howell, along with a multitude of Scotch-Irish and German Palatines, immigrated to the colonies, coming through the port of Philadelphia. William Howell settled in current Bucks County near Philadelphia.

Scotch-Irish-Welch tended to be clannish, independent, and restless. Language of course was a barrier between the different groups of immigrants. Consequently, many of the Scotch-Irish-Welch decided to migrate farther south. Following the "Great Wagon Road," they journeyed through the "Great Appalachian Valley" that runs from New York (Champlain Valley) through Virginia (Shenandoah Valley). The Shenandoah Valley part of the "Great Wagon Road" was originally the "Great Warriors' Trail," established by centuries of migrating bison and Native Americans.

The "Great Wagon Road" was an extremely busy thoroughfare. Lines of wagons traveled north carrying farm produce for northern markets. Large herds of hogs and cattle were also herded north to markets, leaving their dung on the road. The road could be dry and dusty, or wagon wheels could struggle through deep mud. Scotch-Irish-Welch folks found that the German Palatines (also known as "Pennsylvania Dutch") had claimed and settled on the rich farmlands of the Shenandoah Valley. They had to migrate farther south, but the wagon trail became a foot trail. Wagons were abandoned, and the setters carried what they could on the horses' backs and their own backs.

Near present-day Roanoke (also known as "Big Lick"), Virginia, the trail passed through the "Maggoty Gap" of the Blue Ridge Mountains and into the piedmont of North Carolina. The travelers discovered though that this area was already partly settled by immigrants who had entered the colonies through the port of Wilmington, North Carolina. The Scot-Irish-Welch travelers were shocked to find that many of the new residents of Carolina are the hated English. The English persecuted the Scot-Irish-Welch in England, and here they are in Carolina.

James Howell, son of William Howell, along with the others, journeyed west into the mountains of North Carolina in the early 1800s to
escape the English. He was one of the first explorers and settlers of the
Toe River Valley in western North Carolina. The Toe River Valley consists of a series of valleys. The South Toe River valley, along with Cane
River valley, is to the southwest, while the North Toe River flows from the
northeast. The rivers come together and eventually form the Nolichucky
River, the "river of death." Rebel's Creek in present-day Mitchell County
is another one of the small valleys. It has rich farm-lands. Both Howell
and Boone explorers settle in the picturesque and pastoral setting not far
from Boonford.

Interesting for genetic reasons, my great-great-grandfather Robert
Boone marries Naomi Howell, the daughter of James Howell who is my
great-great-great-great grandfather. Sounds like I got a little extra dose of
Howell DNA if everyone indeed stuck to their marriage vows.

Like Robert Boone, John Dillard Howell, my great-great-grandfather, enlists in the Confederate Army in 1861. John Dillard Howell, sta-
tioned on the Potomac River just south of Washington, DC, writes a letter
dated December 26, 1861 to his wife, Sarah:

> *"I am well this morning and Christmas is over and such a Christ-*
> *mas I have never witnessed before. On the evening of the 24th,*
> *the colonel gave the regiment leave to take Christmas and enjoy*
> *themselves as well as they were able. They commenced sending off*
> *after liquor and nearly all got drunk and fought like dogs and cats.*
> *About all our company got drunk and what did not fight wanted*
> *to. But I assure you I was wide awake, cooly sober and tried to*
> *take care of my friends for I did not taste a drop. I never wanted*
> *Christmas to end as bad in my life."*

General Robert E. Lee's army retreats to defend Richmond, Virginia, the capital of the confederacy. Wounded at the Battle of Seven Pines,
just east of Richmond, John Dillard travels in the back of a wagon to the
Chimborazo Hospital and treated there along with 70,000 other wounded soldiers. His penmanship grows increasingly weak and those letters
difficult to read. He dies in July of 1862 at the age of thirty-three and is
buried with two other soldiers in Oakwood Cemetery in Richmond.

These forces of immigration, migration, and war bring Lena Belle
Boone and Jackson Brown Howell together in 1940. As Jack's parents did,
they ride mules to the house of the justice of the peace and sit on the

mules while the justice, standing on his porch, asks them to repeat their vows. Mules are invaluable, it seems.

Lena born the fourth of sixteen children and four step-children, all suffering from the lashes of despair. Based on the old photographs of the family, she and her siblings could easily pose for some of the iconic images of the Great Depression taken by Dorothea Lange (*Migrant Mother*, 1936). Father makes her quit school in the second grade to take care of the other children being born. Nate Boone is a miner. He has three wives, the first two dying in childbirth.

My mother grows up in an era of great scarcity in the Appalachian Mountains. She brushes her teeth for the first fifteen years of her life with a birch twig, frayed at the end. As a child, her Christmas present is typically an apple or an orange. Her younger brothers and sisters played with an inflated hog bladder filled with grains of corn to make a rattle. It is a dearth time. Cracks between the uneven boards on the house allow snow to blow in during the winter. A wood stove in the middle of the house provides some warmth in that immediate area, but bedrooms are icy cold. She sleeps with two sisters. During the night to stay warm, they take turns sleeping in the middle. She dreams of someday living in a "good warm house" on "a piece of flat land."

Beautiful in so many ways, my mother, without a lot of education, develops a few superstitions, along with some hard-won wisdom. After my first daughter, Wendy, is born, we travel from Virginia to see my mother. In the afternoon, Wendy naps in a crib in a bedroom. The adults gather in the family room to "visit" and drink coffee from mugs darkly stained by nearly a quarter of a century of wear. After a while, we notice that Ma, as we called my mother, is not in the room. We go to the bedroom. Ma has Wendy (a few months old) by the heels, holding her upside down, and gently slapping her on the back. "Ma!" I exclaim, "What are you doing?" Calmly, Ma says, "You city folks don't know this". . . continuing to slap Wendy on the back . . . "but these babies, you have to beat the liver off the backbone . . . cause the liver will grow to the backbone and cause all kinds of problems!" Wendy, now an adult, has never had any back or liver problems.

Men frighten my mother, especially "wooly men." A man with long, unkempt hair and a bushy beard might cause her to cross a street to keep from getting too close. When home from college under the hippie culture influence with long hair, she declares that I am "wooly looking." A "wooly looking" man though has hope. He can "clean up" according to my mother, but a "wooly man" she said, will never clean up because he has been that way too long, "set in his ways." Donald Davis, named by many as the world's greatest storyteller, told me, "When I was a child the worst insult my mama could call somebody was a 'Wooly Booger!'"

Some of my mother's superstitions prove beneficial. When I have measles, my medicine is sassafrass tea made from the leaves that my mother gathers deep in the woods. Today, sassafrass tea is touted as a herbal remedy for a variety of disorders (and my measles went away). Every spring, my mother goes down to the banks of the Toe River, digs "yellow root" and makes us a spring tonic. Today, yellow ("yeller" is of course the correct pronunciation) root is popular for its medicinal value, but maybe to be proper one should say "I am going down to the river bank to dig up some Xanthorhiza simplicissima."

Our diet rich in fiber (didn't know it at the time) consists of pinto beans every week-day evening with fried potatoes in the winter and our garden vegetables in the summer. We dig our potatoes in the fall "when the full moon goes down" and put them away in the cellar. They are good until the spring. As her ancestors did, my mother pickles (also popular now) everything she gets her hands on because that is the way we and our ancestors survive without refrigeration. She pickles corn, beans, cucumbers, beets in several large crocks that have alternating layers of salt and cloth.

I don't recall eating fresh seafood until I was a grown man and on a honeymoon in Florida. The mining companies polluted our rivers, and the fish were "not fit to eat." Any other kind of fish or seafood was simply unaffordable. The one exception was when my mother announced one Saturday afternoon that we are in for a surprise: Seafood! With great anticipation, we take our places at the table, and out of the oven comes "Mrs. Paul's Fish Sticks." It was a treat! And for all we knew, that was the seafood being eaten at fancy seafood restaurants in Charleston, South Carolina, and Savannah, Georgia that same evening.

As a boy "eating out" means taking a plate of beans out to the front porch and watching the very occasional car travel up the highway. We have a local "grill," but we never know when it would be open. The owner is an alcoholic, although the locals don't use that term. Instead, they say "He stays on a big drunk." He does not open up if he is "hungover." This is before the day of government restaurant inspectors. Because several people become ill after eating there, the grill earns the name "Tomaine

Tavern" among locals. We didn't want to know that the correct spelling was ptomaine. It wouldn't work as well.

Dining takes a real shot in the arm after the Korean War. A local man, a highly decorated member of the Screaming Eagles of the 101th Airborne Division, falls in love while in Southeast Asia. He and his wife return to start a Chinese restaurant, which is incredible for our area because we don't have many American restaurants. Oriental decorations inside and out make the restaurant look like a palace. People travel for hundreds of miles to eat at Beams. My father says if we are extremely frugal we might go once every three months. We all pitch in to make it happen. My brother once went almost a month without hair-styling Brylcreem to help the cause of eating at Beams. That was a monumental sacrifice for a teenager in those days.

Pathologically shy, father once hid in the woods behind our house for days to avoid jury duty. We took him food, water, and dry blankets every night. Take it from me, social anxiety is a painful disorder. It is bad enough to be in public but torturous to have to speak in public. The body is wracked with anxiety as worse case possible scenarios go through the mind.

Jack, one of the oldest of fourteen children, stops school at the fifth grade to help on the farm. The farm is not mechanized. Fields are plowed with mules. Crops of cabbage and beans are handpicked before being taken to far-away markets. Cows have to be milked, hogs "slopped" with buckets of food scraps and water, water drawn from the well, and firewood has to be cut.

"Emotionally distant" sounds like an understatement for my father. He worked hard at manual labor all day long and then worked evenings for many years to build us a new house. I wanted to play sports but have found myself many times wishing I had spent some time with him and learned some of his skills. We went fishing one time. I fell in and had to be rescued by my father and another man at the river.

For entertainment as a child, I go into the woods, cut a grapevine, and swing like Tarzan. My father brings a rope home from the mines one evening and throws it over a strong limb of an oak tree at the edge of the woods near our house. He fashions a board into a seat, and we have a wonderful swing. I swing high, high enough to fall out backwards if not careful. Swinging through the air kicking out my feet to go higher is one of my best memories.

My father's social anxiety (also called social phobia) might have been caused by a firewood cutting episode. When thirteen, my father receives a striking pocket knife from a relative, payment for some chores done. The pocket knife, something like a Swiss Army Knife with multiple blades and "to die for," is a real status symbol in those days among the boys. Incredibly his brother, Woodrow, was willing to risk death for the knife and agrees to let Jack cut him down out of a tree in exchange for the knife. Why cutting a tree down with his brother up in it appealed so much to Jack, we will never know. But sure enough, Woodrow climbs up an oak tree, and my father chops it down with an ax. When the tree hits the ground, Woodrow is thrown head over heels on the ground, badly bruised but okay. Their father, Troy, beats my father brutally. The beating is severe, life-threatening. Word of the abuse reaches the father of Jack's mother, the other grandfather. John rides his horse to the Howell farm and issues a threat to Troy "if you ever beat that child or any of my grandchildren like that again, I will kill you." At a family gathering over ten years ago, Jack's brother Ray cried when he retold the story of the brutal beating.

My grandfather, Troy Howell, creates one of the most infamous incidents ever in the mountains. He has fields on both sides of the North Toe River. A "swinging bridge" spans the river. Most of the swinging bridges in Western North Carolina are gone, but a few still exist. Swinging bridges are suspended above the river by ropes or, if fortunate, cables. The foot-bridge is narrow, maybe allowing two people to pass. Old wood planks make the floor. Troy, several times a year, moves his cattle from one field to another field crossing the swinging bridge. The cows can barely squeeze across the tight sides of the bridge. Folks for years warned Troy the bridge is not meant to support the weight of several cows at the same time. A storm is coming up one day, and Troy can't find any of his sons to help. Troy rushes several cows across the bridge. About half-way across the bridge, a large cow breaks a board in the floor. The river is swift-flowing and deep below. The next cow steps into the hole created by the broken board and knocks out another board. Unable to climb out of the hole the cow falls into the river below. Another cow approaches the hole in the bridge floor, stops, but the cows behind push the cow into the hole. One cow after another is pushed into the hole and falls into the river below, until five cows, remarkably all alive, are swimming in the river and successfully climb up the bank on the other side after a good bath. My grandfather, unfortunately, was hard on cows and sons.

I don't know if the beating causes my father's social anxiety, but he grows up avoiding human contact as much as possible, working in the local mines and shunning opportunities to work with his merchant brothers in growing local towns. The mines are open-faced. The ore is feldspar, the white substance used to make bathroom sinks, toilets, etc. My father says his favorite job after the dynamite blasting on the side of the mine is to be let down on a rope, swing through the air, and knock off the loose rocks and small boulders from the sides of the cliff with a big, sturdy stick. The other workers could then safely come in below and scoop up the valuable ore into buckets. His friends use to tease him, "Jack with those skills you could always go and join the circus!"

Not as dangerous as underground coal mining, danger still lurks around open-faced mines. I remember the terror I feel when a knock rattles the door one cold rainy night. Bill Gibson, my father's best friend, working the second shift at the mine, in his bulldozer goes off the wooden bridge that spans the raging North Toe River. Men are going house to house knocking on doors and asking for mine company employees and anyone that could help find Bill Gibson. The rains cause the river to swell over its banks. Bill's body is found miles downriver. I could tell my extremely introverted father is hurt deeply. Not one for building relationships, he finally has a friend, and now Bill is swept away by a raging river.

Give the Devil His Due!

"... the Lord our God is a jealous God,
visiting the iniquity of the father upon the children ..."

EXODUS 20:5

AN ACCUSATION OF MURDER falls on Jack Howell as a young man. He turns fifteen and develops an interest in young women. Without a drivers' license or a car, he walks up the only road (NC 80) that goes through Boonford to "call upon" a young woman. Buster Wilson permits Jack to see his daughter, Rose Wilson, but they cannot leave the property. Shy to the bone, Jack cannot resist his attraction to Rose. Going to her house is the hardest thing he has ever done. Rose, also fifteen, is already in full blossom. Tall, charming, with striking pale blue eyes, her blonde hair shines as if lightly kissed by the sun. She still has a childlike giggle. Sitting in the swing on the front porch on this chilly March night, they cuddle close together. Stepping outside, her father announces that it is time for them to say goodnight. Rose and Jack go through their goodbye rituals, and Jack starts walking down the road toward home.

As Jack Howell walks down the road on that moonless night, he hears the distant bark of a dog and then a series of loud gunshots. In a rural area especially in that day, gunshots are not that unusual, so Jack does not think much about it. Jack notices the lights from kerosene lanterns swinging in the gentle breeze at Winn Gouge's house and barn. Electricity has not made it to Boonford yet. Not unusual, but what catches Jack's eye is that the front door of the house is open (on this cold night) and the double doors of the barn are wide open. Curious, Jack walks over to the house and knocks on the door. They don't want their door open like this, he thinks. No one answers his knock, so he walks over to the barn. Inside on the dusty floor, staring at the tall ceiling with exposed rafters is Winn Gouge and Hassie, his wife. Both are dead, shot several times in the chest.

Buster Wilson hears the shots as well and figures they came from the Gouge home. His car pulls in about the same time Jack walks into the barn. They both are aghast at the bloody scene. Minutes later, the county sheriff who happens to be patrolling the area pulls up to the barn. Jack and Buster explain they just arrived as well and are dumbfounded by the scene. Modern criminal forensics would never allow this, but the sheriff asks Jack and Buster to help move the bodies over to the house "where they belong." When the gory task is completed, Jack explains that he is long overdue at home and does not want to worry his mother. The sheriff thanks him for his help, and Jack heads back down the road toward home.

About this time, the deputy sheriff, having received a call to come as a backup to the murder scene, comes up the road. He slams on the brakes when he sees Jack on the side of the road. He throws open the car door, jumps out, and pulls his revolver, pointing it straight at Jack. "Murderer, turn around and get your hands behind your back." The deputy puts cuffs on Jack and pushes him into the back seat of the cruiser. "I didn't do anything!" Jack protests. When Jack sits, the deputy's door is open and the overhead light is on. That is when Jack notices he is covered with blood. It is Winn Gouge's blood that he of course got on him when moving the bodies. The deputy jumps in the car and roars away. After pulling into the Gouge house, the deputy finds the sheriff and proudly proclaims, "I have the killer." The sheriff and Buster Jones explain to the deputy that Jack helped move the bodies and thus the bloody clothes.

Jack, up early the next day, heads through a rising morning mist to the field for a day of picking beans. His mother, Elsie, comes into the room Jack shares with five brothers to get their dirty clothes. Elsie and daughters are going down to the river with washboards to do the semi-weekly laundry. Elsie eyes in shock the bloody clothes on the floor, for she has heard earlier that morning about the murders. "Jack!" she screams, "He murdered Winn Gouge!" The younger siblings, those not old enough to be working in the fields, rush into the room, and start screaming. El-sie rushes out to the field and tells Troy, her husband, about the bloody clothes. Jack, barefooted, is picking beans. Troy yells, "Jack, get over here right now!" Jack explains the bloody clothes, and everyone settles down. The murder case is never solved. The murderer or murderers by now have gone to their graves with their bloody secrets.

Although Jack and I share an abundance of traumatic events in our young lives, from what I understand, at least part of social anxiety disorder is caused by genetics, "the shy gene" they call it. According to Darwin's evolutionary theories and brain scientists, those of us with the shy gene are fortunate to be around. "Natural selection" favors the bold and aggressive. Reluctant males especially could be left behind in the aggressive battles for food and mates that would result in continuing the species. There are other factors for me. My father did not "beat me within an inch of my life" as his father did, but he could be abusive (although in that day it was mild abuse compared to what happened to some kids). The abuse came from my father as a delayed response. My father said I was a "smart-aleck," and indeed I could be. I had at least a touch of ADHD's impulsive speech quality. Growing up I never have much to say, but when I do, it always seems to be the wrong thing. I say some smart-alecky thing to my father or just in general. A few minutes pass. Then I feel a blunt, stinging sensation, a slap to the back of my head, or an upward thrust of my body caused by a serious kick to my posterior. My brain quickly puts together I have said something "smart-alecky" a few minutes earlier, but in the moment it is painful and confusing.

Other traumatic events probably caused my social anxiety and near PTSD symptoms. Part of my career is spent as a licensed professional counselor. We learned to be diagnosed with PTSD a person did not have to receive directly the trauma. A person witnessing a traumatic event is eligible for the PTSD diagnosis.

In one of my earliest memories, I play out back between our house and the old barn. We have chickens to lay eggs, as opposed to some who preferred guinea or duck eggs. We have a rooster as well. A rooster is not needed for the hens to lay eggs. If you want chicks, you need a rooster to fertilize the eggs. I am probably three or four at the time. The world is a wonderful, safe place as I walk toward the barn with my mother who has invited me to go with her to gather eggs. I make a mistake. I get distracted by an interesting rock on the ground and fall behind. Suddenly without warning the rooster flies into my face! Screeching and clawing at my face! I am getting a floggin'. The rooster is protecting his harem. My mother is too large for the rooster to attack, but a little boy that falls behind is a perfect target. I can still feel the terror to this day. I did not know what was happening at first. Brown and red feathers are all in my face. Flapping wings send shoots of air past my ears . . . Whoosh! Whoosh! I feel the cuts opening on my face and blood running down. Instinctively, I go down on the ground to protect myself, covering my head with my arms. My mother turns around, runs back, and says, "Get! Get! Get out of here, you durn rooster!" The rooster retreats, and my mother puts her loving arms around a crying, terrified little boy.

Later in psychotherapy, a requirement in training for licensed pastoral psychotherapist, I discover I am not only terrified by the floggin' but intensely angry at that damn rooster. That shrieking bird-beast shattered my sense of safety that Maslow (Hierarchical of Needs Pyramid) says I needed for healthy psycho-social development. I should have done what Ruby Thewes, played by Renee Zellwegger in *Cold Mountain*, does when confronted by an aggressive rooster. She says, "I hate a floggin' rooster" to Ada Monroe (Nicole Kidman) and proceeds to "wring the rooster's neck" and declares, "Let's put him in a pot!" I never "wrung a rooster or chicken's neck," but I saw my grandmother do it several times. It was quick, decisive, and probably the easiest death for the fowl.[1]

With no neighborhood kids to play with, I want a dog. A Saturday morning, my mother takes me to Penland, a little community in Mitchell County that is also home to Penland School of Craft (an internationally known school for craft education managed by people "from off somewhere" that the locals called "communists" and the rumor is they practice "yoga," a non-Christian cult activity).

My mother works with a woman, living near Penland, who has a dog with puppies ready to be adopted. I am so excited as we get out of the car. My mother's friend comes out to meet us. Driving over in the car, my mother warned me that her friend "always looks like an unmade bed" that she never combs her hair or puts on makeup or lipstick and her clothes are misfit and wrinkled. I don't care. I am focused on getting a puppy, a friend, a playmate. Laser-focused I head for the dog house where the puppies are. The mother dog is across the yard but sees me headed to her pups. I am so focused on the dog house that I don't see her coming. Pain sears in my back thigh. My mother screams. The mother dog lets go, but my leg hurts like a hundred bee stings. We leave with a puppy. I name him Champ.

Wonderful Champ, we run, wrestle, and nap together. A second cousin who has recently obtained his driver's license develops a reputation of intentionally running over dogs. My brother, about the same age as the dog slayer, swears that Velmer Howell goes out about every day looking for dogs to hit. We live close enough to the road that I worry about this. One sunny, warm afternoon I can't find Champ. I look all around our house, but he is not there. I go down to the road, and my heart breaks. Champ is in the ditch and bleeding. A car hit him. Was it Velmer? We never knew for sure, but we suspected this Howell. I was angry enough to wish him Hell bound as per Pastor Leroy's edict.

I participate in the annual "hog killin." Garrison Keillor says when he was growing up in Minnesota that a ritual into "manhood" was first-time permission to drive the tractor that pulled the manure spreader. He recalls beaming with pride as the tractor went over the fields and the manure that fell on him was a badge of honor. For our Appalachian community participating in the annual hog killing was the same rite of passage.

In the fall, after the annual potato digging and storing in the cellar for the coming winter, winds pick up, and the temperature drops. Fallen brown leaves blow across our driveway and look like a stampede of tiny miniature bison. When the crescent moon shines, according to the old-timers, "the blood is in the foot" and the perfect time for "hog killin." The older men in the community planned all of their farming activities based on phases of the moon, and somehow a crescent moon caused a flow of blood in the animal that resulted in optimum meat flavor.

We fed the innocent hog with scraps from the table and store-bought feed through the spring and summer. But this cool, crisp late autumn day would be like no other for this well-nourished animal. We rise before the sun and start the fire that boils water in the large tub sitting on a round pile of rocks and above the fire. The animal loses its life to a twenty-two caliber bullet between the eyes. Some of the bigger hogs require more than one shot. My father pre-prepares a strong hickory stick he has cut in the woods, four feet long and sharpened on each end. The stick goes through each side of the hog's rear ankles. A rope is secured to the middle of the stick, and the rope is attached to a pulley that lifts the animal upside down. It is my job then to bring buckets of boiling water from the large tub and pour over the carcass. The hot water softens the hair on the skin of the hog and makes it easier for us to scrap the hair off with big butcher knives. Then like his ancestors for centuries before him, my father disembowels the generous creature who would soon give us his flesh for our sustenance. With surgeon-like precision my father removes unwanted (not many) organs. Skillfully, he slices the meat that is called side-meat or streaked meat (bacon), pork chops, and hams. Evening comes, and the feast of the hog is celebrated. My mother cooks a few vegetables, but we mostly sample from the meats gifted to us by our hog. The meats are wrapped, labeled, and stored in the freezer to keep us alive during the long, cold, hard mountain winter. When times are really hard, we eat "chitlins." Simply put, the hog's large intestines are removed, cleaned, battered, and fried. Vinegar was often drizzled over the lumpy, pancake-looking entree. Chitlins were a common food for the poor of medieval Europe. In *Tess of the D'Uurbevilles,* Thomas Hardy wrote of chitlins. As a pescatarian now, I am not proud of my part in the taking of this life in such a gruesome manner, but it was a necessary brutality at the time.

Gangs of Boonford!

"I am good but not an angel."
MARILYN MONROE

LESTER MURDOCK FATHERS TWO boys, Cole and Creed, who are the muscle of their bootlegging operation. Lester, the boys, and his wife Kitty live in a "trailer home" stuck on the side of a mountain and beside an abandoned tunnel mine. The once white but now yellow-stained trailer's gutters hang loosely from each end. Cole and Creed put large dents over the years in the side of the trailer with thrown balls and rocks.

Kitty catches Lester in bed with a local teenage girl when she returns to the trailer earlier than expected from a trip into town. Kitty has long been a believer in the old wisdom saying, "Spare the rod and spoil the child." Well, in this case, it is "spare the ax and spoil Lester." Grabbing an ax, she swings and slices off Lester's arm. Lester survives but without his arm that Kitty throws into the cook-stove's wood fire.

Cole and Creed born mean to the bone, look for mischief. Lester crawls under their trailer to look for a dead smelly rat one afternoon while Kitty visits a sister. Eight-year-old Cole, and Creed, a year younger, latch the crawl space door, and their father is trapped under the trailer for hours, screaming and cursing at his sons, who are laughing the entire time while sitting in lawn chairs just a few feet away. Kitty holds each boy while Lester beats them with his belt. It only makes them meaner.

The following year Kitty sits in the privy (outdoor toilet). The outhouse is not well attached to the ground and simply sits over the smelly hole in the ground. Cole and Creed push the outhouse over, breaking their mother's arm. Another beating from Lester solidifies their socio-pathic behavior.

Lester possibly descended from Melungeons. Technically a tri-racial ethnic group, Melungeons are thought to be descendants of ship-wrecked Portuguese sailors on the North Carolina coast who interbreed with Native Americans, escaped African slaves, and, some have theorized, members of the Lost Colony. Lester, like some others in the area, is whispered to be Melungeon and that explained his oily, curly hair, light brown skin, and deep dark eyes. He has a smile that lifts the left side of his face and gives him a devilish appearance. However, the striking feature for Lester now is his missing arm. He always wears bib overalls, a striped baseball-type hat often worn by railroad engineers, and long sleeve shirts, even though one sleeve has no arm in it. I recall seeing terrified young children who for the first time see a blast of wind take Lester's armless sleeve up into the air and whirl it around. For Lester, this is great entertainment, seeing children with eyes big as saucers and about to come out of their heads.

Yancey county is "dry," meaning no alcohol sales of any kind are permitted. If one makes the necessary contribution to the local sheriff's "poverty relief fund," one can quietly resell beer, wine, and liquor pur-chased from a "wet" county. But competition is fierce for the resell mar-ket. If a bootlegger is established in an area, it means war if someone tries to move in on the lucrative business with at least 100 percent markup. The Murdocks furiously protect their territory

A startup operation called the "Razor Blade Gang" challenges the Murdocks. A young man, Kermit Gurley, and an attractive young wom-an, Jolene Banks, both high school dropouts, try to establish a foothold in the Murdocks's market. It is rumored their weapons of choice are long straight razors, like barbers use for shaving customers. The titillating part of the rumor for the local men is that Jolene keeps her straight razor between her breasts. Jolene boasts she "will wear Cole Murdock's balls as earrings." The Razor Blade Gang raids the Murdock's liquor warehouse on a Saturday night and takes most of their liquor. The raid is a brazen act for the warehouse is the abandoned tunnel mine, a hundred yards from Lester Murdock's trailer.

Murdocks promise swift, harsh retribution, like never seen before, upon the Razor Blade Gang. A frightened Jolene takes the gang's car and flees to family in Madison County. Kermit tries to escape on foot. Cole heads to the next alcohol selling county to replenish the liquor for the Sunday afternoon sales that will come after church is dismissed.

A quiet Sunday morning, five years old, I eat my cereal at the kitchen table and watch squirrels chase each other up and down a massive oak tree. My mother screams from the front room, "He's going to kill him! God help us! He's going to beat him to death!" I race to the front room, and, out the window, I see the unfolding, horrifying event. We live on the side of the mountain, looking down on the road below. We don't have any neighbors. Perched on the other side of the road is one lonely abandoned house. A creek peacefully flows between the road and the other house.

In the road below Cole Murdock attempts murder. Cole, headed to the next county, comes around the curve below our house. Walking in front of our house is Kermit Gurley, Razor Blade Gang member. Cole spots the liquor thief. The car's momentum takes him past Kermit. Slamming on the brakes, Cole throws the transmission into reverse, trying to run over Kermit. Cole can't find him in his rearview mirror, so he opens the door attempting to see his victim. He sees him, swerves to hit him, but he is leaning the wrong way and falls out of the car. The car slows down and settles softly in the ditch. Cole jumps to his feet, screaming, "I am going to kill you, you goddamn son of a bitch!" Cole catches up and delivers blow after blow to the head and torso of his victim. The young man reels from the blows and falls backward into the road ditch. Cole kicks him several times and then shouts at him, "I'm going to get my gun and kill you." While Cole goes for the gun in the car, Kermit jumps up and runs away.

As a young child, I watch this in unbelievable, shaking horror, for the beaten Kermit is running toward our house! He gets to the door and knocks thunderously. "Let me in! Help me! He is going to kill me!" I couldn't believe it when my father opens the door and tells Kermit to hide in the closet. Cole is now coming up the hill with his gun. "What is going to happen? What is my father going to do?" I wonder in absolute terror. Stunned, I see Cole stop when he sees my father in the doorway, puts the pistol behind his back, and says "Jack, I am sorry to have bothered you." He turns, walks down the hillside, gets in his car, and speeds away to complete his mission of restocking the liquor supplies.

Why Cole stopped coming up the hill always puzzled me until now. My unarmed father shelters his bitter enemy. Only now as I write this does it dawn on me that Cole did not want to kill or even offend one of his best customers, my father!

Years later, we think the Murdock clan is wiped out. Bill Ballew is a dapper little man in his late seventies. He moved to the area from

Washington, DC, claiming to be a retired secret service agent, having protected Roosevelt and Churchill. No one believed his story, figuring he was probably a government bean-counter in some agency in DC. Bill likes to talk but never opens his mouth wide enough. His speech is a mumbled, rush of words. Locals call him Mumbling Bill. Every day he walks to my Uncle's store. His excursions are remarkable for he is as bow-legged as a person can be and still walk. Every step is a gravity-defying balancing feat, and it is painful to watch him walk. He is always superbly dressed: straw hat, bowtie, pleated pants, and sometimes white shoes. We figure he does not get out much. His wife died many years ago. He cannot drive a car. So, when he walks to the store, he puts on his finest clothes.

When he steps into the store on this particular day, he is nearly breathless. His legs are too arthritic to run, but he has walked as fast as possible. With his cane in his right hand, he raises his left hand as he enters the double doors of the store, doors left open during the summer. Mumbling Bill wants everyone to pay attention, "A boo-hoo boys, a boo-hoo!. Listen up! The Murdocks have buck-headed out of Boonford and killed a whole generation! They're all dead!" We all know Mumbling Bill is subject to exaggeration. But we soon find out there is something to his story. There has been a wreck, and such a wreck that one would expect considerable human carnage. Uncle sends me to check out the scene of the wreck.

Highway 80 from Boonford snakes over a mountain and after a rapid descent intersects with the old 19-E that goes between Burnsville and Spruce Pine. The new 19-E highway runs parallel to the old 19-E. Uncle's store is on the new highway, but Mumbling Bill always walks down the old road since there is less traffic. He arrives at the intersection of old 19-E and steep Highway 80 just after the Murdocks have an epic car wreck, crashing down the road in their red Dodge Charger like a rollercoaster with no brakes. Maybe their brakes give way coming down the mountain? Or maybe they have too much speed for when they come to the "T" intersection of 19-E and 80, they cannot make the turn. The red Charger goes over on its side, scoots along the side of the road, strikes a huge old stump, and flips into the air. Mumbling Bill witnesses the circus-like crash and presumes that all the occupants must be dead. He heads on to Uncle's store with the chilling proclamation.

At this point, however, the Murdocks prove once again their invincibility. They all survive the spectacle and walk away. It appears that neither negligence, bad fortune, nor fate can deter their grip on the area.

Known for one other adventure, Mumbling Bill loves musician Arthur Smith who has a television program. Charlotte television station WBT broadcasts "Arthur Smith and the Crackerjacks" (a bluegrass band) each day. Not many people get that station in the mountains, but the few who do have lots of guests when the show airs. Although he does not receive the channel, Mumbling Bill never misses a show. He is seen knocking on someone's door every day at noon when the show airs. The Crackerjacks are brother Ralph Smith, Tommy Faile, Wayne "Skeeter" Haas, and others.

"Arthur Smith and the Crackerjacks" schedule a concert in Asheville for 7:00 PM on a Wednesday evening. It is a dream for Mumbling Bill to attend. Since he does not have a car, he catches the 9:25 AM (and only) Greyhound bus to Asheville. He spends the day outside the Civic Center Coliseum where the concert will take place. He munches on a jelly biscuit and an apple from his coat pocket during the afternoon. First in line to buy a ticket, he purchases a great seat near the front. By the time the concert starts, the 5:15 PM bus has long departed. Mumbling Bill has no way to get home, but he hatches a clever plan.

Mumbling Bill leaves the concert early, shuffles his way out a side door, and finds the large bus with a sign on it that says "Arthur Smith and the Crackerjacks." Outside the bus, the driver smokes a cigarette with his back to the bus. Seizing the opportunity, Mumbling Bill slips through the open door of the bus, limps up the short set of steps and down the aisle of the dark bus. The concert is over, fans exit, and band members make their way to the bus. When the driver senses the band is about to arrive, he enters the bus and turns on the interior lights. Mumbling Bill is outstretched on the back seat, a long one-row seat. The back seat is always reserved for Wayne "Skeeter" Haas. Other band members enter the bus and take their normal seats. Arthur sits in the front row. Wayne Haas makes his way to the rear of the bus. Shocked and then angry, he sees the old man stretched out on the back seat. Impulsively, Skeeter Haas grabs Mumbling Bill. Before Skeeter can say anything, Mumbling Bill screams, "Arthur, Arthur, help me! I've been down with gout and still came!" The next day, the *Asheville Times*, the afternoon newspaper, has a front-page story: "Man Claiming To Be Former Secret Service Agent Found Hiding on Arthur Smith's Bus." At Uncle's store, none of the elderly men who gather there can read. I read to them the story of Mumbling Bill, and they shake their heads in amazement.

Cole and The King of Rock and Roll!

"It is strange to be known so universally
and yet to be so lonely."

ALBERT EINSTEIN

THE MURDOCKS EXPERIENCE AN incredible brush with fame. Elvis visits Burnsville, but no one knows why? The polio pandemic sweeps the nation. People are skeptical of the Salk polio vaccine. On "The Ed Sullivan Show", Elvis rolls up his right shirt sleeve and leads America in the way of the polio vaccine. It is not far from Nashville to western North Carolina. For whatever reason, Elvis comes to town, maybe to rest up from touring and vaccine injection, and stays at the famous Nu Wray Inn.

Nu Wray Inn still sits on the town square, and folks, sure enough, come from cities like Charlotte and Atlanta to stay because of its small-town, mountain charm. Other famous visitors were Mark Twain, Jimmy Carter, Thomas Wolfe, and Christopher Reeves. There were no televisions, no radios, and people say it is like going back in time. Old planks creak. Rooms have high ceilings and antique furnishings. The Inn has a breakfast like none ever beheld in the mountains. We did not know at the time, but the owners were from Southampton, British Isles. It is an English breakfast with bacon, sausages, eggs, black pudding, baked beans, tomatoes, and mushrooms. For us at home, a fancy breakfast is eggs and maybe some "side meat" or "streaked meat" (a form of home-cured bacon, now called "pork-belly" in fine restaurants).

At the Inn, folks still talk about Elvis sneaking down from his room in the middle of the night and making a peanut butter and banana sandwich in the inn kitchen. Elvis had the English breakfast, and he also had a late-night visit from a notable local. Cole's young cousin, who proudly sports some peach fuzz for a beard, washes dishes at the Inn and calls Cole, "You'uns want to know something citing?" "Citing" was a lazy way of saying "exciting" in the mountains. "Hod-damn Elvis is staying here. I swear it! I ain't posed to tell nobody, but he's here. Maybelline at the front desk pissed in her bloomers when Elvis checked in."

Cole says, "Cousin, I'll bring you a fifth of good liquor if you get me his room number, what you say?" After a few moments of pause and reflection, Cousin says, "I ain't had no good liquor lately. Okay but don't tell nobody, not a soul, you hear!"

About 10:30 PM, Cole, dressed in his best, a light blue polyester leisure suit, parks about two blocks away on a side street. The moonless night is pitch black, and the tip of Cole's lit cigarette glows in the dark as he walks toward the Inn. His heels click on the old sidewalk as he walks through the crisp air. He knows where the service door is at the rear of the ancient building. Looking both ways, he makes sure no one sees him grabs the cold knob, and pulls the awkward fitting rear door open, although he does see curtains pulled together in the window above him. As the hinges groan, he steps inside. A frightened white cat streaks down the hall, but the coast is clear. Elvis is in Room 9. Cousin told Cole that Elvis's driver is in a separate room. Cole walks slowly and cautiously down the hall. The old wood floors squeak and moan. Room 9 looms on the left. Checking again for anyone that might be in the hall, and finding no one, he knocks on the door. No answer. He knocks again.

"Who is it?"

Sounds like Elvis! Cole thinks as excitement makes his skin tingle.

"Delivery!" Cole declares as his eyes widen.

"Just leave it there," Elvis says.

Cole sits the brown bag containing a fifth of liquor down outside the door. Cole steps to one side and puts his back against the hall wall. The door rattles open. The heavy smell of cigar smoke drifts toward Cole. Elvis sees the bag on the floor. He picks it up, peaks inside, and a curious smile comes on his face. He still has not spotted Cole. Seeing his hero only a couple of feet away, Cole turns fully toward Elvis. Elvis jumps back, stumbling slightly.

"Who are you?" an alarmed Elvis demands as his deep blue eyes drill into Cole.

"I'm Cole. Great fan of yours." And getting quickly to the point before Elvis loses patience, "I brought you a little Burnsville welcoming present."

"Nice of you, but people aren't supposed to know I'm here!" Elvis says with apprehension.

"I know." says Cole as he drops his head a little in embarrassment. "My cousin works here and told me about you. And listen. My phone number is on the bag. If you need some more liquor, just call. Won't cost you nuttin."

"Thanks!" says Elvis and reaches out for a handshake! Cole extends his hand as his jaw drops. Cole feels the softest hands he has ever touched, nothing like the calloused hands of the mill workers and farmworkers of this area. They are the soft, pampered hands of the world's most popular musician at the time.

Elvis and Cole say their goodbyes. Cole, not worrying about a creaking hall floor or if anyone sees him, strides proudly out the front door of the Inn and up the two blocks to his car. Cole controls his exuberance only a few steps up the street, and then lets out a scream of pure joy that rattles the windows of the old Inn, "Son of a bitch! . . . I met Elvis!"

Back in his car, Cole rewards himself with big gulps from his own brown bag, the best liquor he knows of, Jack Daniels. He streaks through the night and back to Boonford.

Cole cannot contain himself. He wants to share his incredible experience, but most folks are in bed. Unlike the entrepreneur Cole, they have real jobs in mines and factories. They get up early. Cole finds an exception. Zola Briggs works the late dinner shift as a short-order cook at Lil'Smoky Drive-Inn in Burnsville. Not home long, her lights are on. Thinking Zola wants to know his good fortune, Cole pulls into her dirt driveway. He blows the horn. Cole's alcohol-infused adrenaline rush has him thinking everyone will want to know about The King.

Zola had "good raizen" and consequently "good manners." So she opens the front door and shields her eyes from the bright lights of the headlights. Zola recognizes Cole and knows he usually means trouble. She asks, "Can I help you?" Rolling down his window, Cole shouts, "I've seen Elvis! He's at the Nu Wray Inn! Yep, took him a fifth of liquor, handed it to him right at his room. He's real nice and all. Damn, I met Elvis! I can't believe it!" Zola forces a smile and says "Thank you. Thank you for letting us know." She steps back into the house and shuts her door.

Back on the highway, Cole sees only dark houses, except for old man Reuben Sparks's house, way up on a hill. Ole Reuben, as they call him, is in his late eighties. His wife died a few years ago. All their neighbors have indoor plumbing by now, but Reuben and Betty say they are just fine without it. The real reason is they barely have enough money to buy food. Reuben now cooks for himself. For supper that day he consumes leftovers from over a week ago. "Dinner" is the mid-day meal with "supper" in the evening. Only city folks "from off somewhere" eat "lunch."

Reuben's house smells like old, unwashed socks. Dirty pots and pans fill his sink. A skinny tan cat snoozes beside his bed. Reuben can't sleep as the bacteria-infested leftovers give him severe intestinal contractions. He wakes, his belly about to explode. Reuben, an old-timer, wears even during the summer, long-sleeved and full-length insulated underwear. Although originally white, his "long-johns" glow an aged mustard-yellow. In his "johns" as they are called, he motors across his yard as the cold air stings his skin. His "outhouse" smells like Satan's toilet. Reuben's outhouse is slightly larger than a phone booth, with weather-worn boards and a rusty tin roof. The fragile-looking structure sits over a deep open hole in the earth that has been the septic tank for Reuben's family for generations.

Reuben makes it just in time. The great thing about "johns" is the drop-flap in the back. Reuben lowers the flap, sits over the hole, and the rest of his long-johns keep him warm. If you are "well-off" (have money) in the mountains, you probably have a two-hole outdoor john. Reuben just has one hole, but that's all he needs now. If you are "well-off," you scrape your rectum with upscale, smooth pages of the creme de la creme *Spiegel* catalog. Regular folks like Reuben use the rough cheaper paper from the *Sears-Roebuck* catalog or maybe the "funny pages" (comics) of the local newspaper.

With sweat on his brow, Reuben gets some relief sitting on the wooden boards with the big hole cut in the middle and a big stinky mess down below. About that time, Cole, seeing the lights on at Reuben Sparks's pulls into the driveway, blows the horn, and screams, "I met Elvis! I met Elvis!" Reuben is a frequent customer at Murdock's and knows Cole well. With one foot, he reaches up and pushes the outhouse door open.

"Cole, I'm over here in a bad way. Somethin' festering in my bowels." Reuben says with a shaky, weak voice.

Cole exclaims, "Elvis is at the Nu Wray Inn. I went to his room. Gave him a fifth of liquor. I did! He even shook my hand. Hell, I might not ever wash it again!"

"You're going to be famous Cole. I can't come out though. I got a real bad case of the runs. But thanks for letting me know." says Reuben.

"I started to ask him to sing "Don't Be Cruel", but I lost my nerve." laughed Cole.

The next morning, my father told us, "Cole Murdock came by here last night . . ." We all held our breaths because Cole usually means bad news. "He blew his horn. So I went out on the porch. He told me he met Elvis last night at the Nu Wray." We relaxed with relief as my father told us the rest of the story.

To this day, the Nu Wray Inn calls Room 9 the "Elvis Room." Elvis lives on in the hearts of his followers. Cole Murdock lives on in the scarred psyches of children who grew up in his decades of bootlegging, lawlessness, and terror in Boonford. The Murdocks were as feared as MS-13 today.

Cole died a few years ago. His liver was apparently incredibly strong to survive all that booze to an old age. He lived in an old, vine-covered, school bus. During an extremely cold night and after heavy drinking at a friend's house, he returned to the school bus home, pried open the double doors of the bus, started up the steps inside the bus. Stumbling, he fell forward with his neck settling between the gear shift lever and the parking brake lever, side by side in the raised floor of the bus. Apparently, he dangled there for a time, his legs hanging down the steps, and unable to free himself. He freezes to death, a terrible death for anyone.

Cole's brother, Creed, attempts suicide. The locals say Creed "lusts after every woman he sees" and has a sexual relationship with a neighbor's teenage daughter. Enoch Lloyd, the father, learns of the predatory affair. Enoch walks to Creed's house, rifle under his arm. After the knock, Creed opens the door. Enoch fires. An expert hunter and marksman, Enoch has aimed at Creed's genitals and surgically removes with one bullet Creed's manhood.

Hospitalized, Creed recovers, minus his "jewels." Creed's sexual abilities have always been a large part of his identity. Now he is emotionally devastated and can't think of any reason to live. Driving home and despondent, he stops at Uncle's store. Creed enters the store, stands silently for a few minutes, and says, "I ain't got nuttin to live fer. I'm goin home and blow the hell out of everything." Turning, he walks away, climbs into his beat-up, blue Rambler, and heads home.

Word spreads from the customers in the store to the neighborhood residents that Creed plans to blow himself up. Estelle Crow shares a "party" telephone line with six other houses. Estelle picks up the phone to call her friend Queenie Bowditch about Creed's explosive plans. On the shared line, Ora Willis and Lovina Jones talk about the bake sale at the church on Saturday. Ora and Lovina hear the click of another person joining the "party line." Normally, another click follows as the third and uninvited party politely hangs up the receiver. This time Estelle breaks into the conversation, "You'uns heard about Creed Murdock? Goin to blow himself up in a few minutes. Silas and I headed over there right now. You gotta come too!" And she hangs up.

Dozens of people jump in their cars and head to Creed's place. Cars soon line the dirt road in front of Creed's mobile home. People are out of their cars but safely on the opposite side of the car from Creed's place, using their cars as shields. My father drives our car as we go down the main road that passes by the side road where all the cars are parked. "Daddy, what's going on over there?" I ask. "I don't know, but we're going home. That's Creed Murdock's place, and trouble always follows him." My father states strongly.

Shutting all the windows, Creed turns on the propane gas at the stove in the tiny kitchen. Sheriff Mozell Tolley and his deputies with blue lights flashing arrive in a cloud of dust. The sheriff gets out of his car, puts on his white cowboy-like hat, and walks toward the trailer. After a knock on the door, what follows is an encounter much like Butch Cassidy and E. C. Woodcock in the classic film *Butch Cassidy and the Sundance Kid*.

Just like Butch (Paul Newman playing Robert Leroy Parker) pleads with "Woodcock" (the resistant employee in the locked boxcar) to open the door and "save himself," Sheriff Mozell Tolley passionately asks Creed to open the door. Sheriff Tolley smells gas seeping out from around the edges of the door. He backs up and tells his deputies to start throwing rocks at the windows exclaiming, "the fool goin' to do it . . . he's goin' to blow himself up!"

In *Butch Cassidy and the Sundance Kid*, the dynamite explodes and the entire boxcar is destroyed, save "Woodcock." Pieces of the boxcar and paper-money float through the air. A member of the band of thieves says, "Think you used enough dynamite there, Butch?"[2]

Creed goes to the other end of the mobile home, enters the bathroom, and sits on the toilet. With the smell of gas all around him and figuring there is enough gas to blow the trailer to smithereens, Creed flips his Bic lighter. Boom! The trailer rips into pieces. Fragments of wood, siding, furniture fly into the air. The debris and dust settle. With the sides and roof of the trailer gone, Sheriff Tolley, the deputies, and the spectators see Creed Murdock sitting on the toilet, clothes blown away, badly burned, covered in black soot, but alive.

Paladin and Stingy Smith

"Stingy people have often been forced to give when they were very, very young, when they weren't ready."

FRED ROGERS

IN ADDITION TO ELVIS and Mark Twain, more famous people visit the area. For several summers as a teenager, I work for my uncle in his country store. His store is stocked like so many in the mountains with essentials: bread, milk, bananas, apples, canned items, and other non-food essentials like nails, rope, and fishing supplies. A display counter in the front of the store offers large jars of pickled pigs' feet, pickled eggs, and pickled sausage. It was often my job to reach down in the jars with a long extended fork, pull out a pig's foot, wrap it in paper, and hand it to a hungry, just off-work mill hand. In the back of the store, hams hung from the exposed rafters. Uncle bought the hams from local farmers and let them cure in the rear of the store for resale. A ham, as it cures, develops a crust of green mold on the outside. The ham is perfectly fine, but often a person not knowing the fine science of ham curing is taken aback by the sight of the moldy flesh hanging from the ceiling.

With my uncle and father, I sense a clear generational and coming cultural divide. Uncle, my father, and all of the men of the World War II generation comb their hair back often kept in place with greasy creams like Brylcreem or Pomade. Most of them look like James Dean, Clark Gable or Cary Grant. In a generational act of individuation, we wash our hair every day to keep a soft, dry look and let our hair fall down toward our eyes and ears. In a few years, we let our hair grow even longer to look like "The Beatles" or Mick Jagger of the "Rolling Stones." Societies often

33

judge men by the length of their hair, and hair-style was once thought to be a window into the soul. In colonial times, men who had long locks were suspected of having non-Christian ways. Upright rigid hair meant the man was rigid and harsh while a part in the middle meant weakness. North Korea to this day requires a socialist (short) hairstyle for all men. So it should not have been surprising that we were viewed suspiciously when we let our hair grow out.

Uncle, like several of my aunts and uncles, struggles with narco-lepsy. Part of my job, although no one ever told me to do it, is to keep Uncle awake. It is a hot summer day. No one has air conditioning. We open windows and doors, trying to stay cool. Uncle sends me to the feed room in the basement of the store. He stocks pig feed and horse feed in fifty and hundred-pound bags. Customers can drive around the store to the lower level where I load the bags on their trucks.

Sometimes Uncle sends me down to move bags around. One day he wants me to put all the fifty pound bags by the door, and the next day he wants me to move the fifty pound bags away from the door and put one-hundred pound bags by the door. He always tells me to do this in the middle of the afternoon. Business in the upper level of the store where the groceries are, with the gas pumps outside, is slow in the middle of the afternoon. Things pick up after 3:30 PM when the mill and mine workers get off work and come by for milk, bread, baloney, and "hoop" cheese, a round of cheese as big as some present-day cocktail tables tops. We cut off big chunks for our customers. But prior to the 3:30 PM rush hour Uncle sends me down to the lower level for the mind-less and essentially useless moving of the feed bags. It dawns on me one day, he does this so he can get some uninterrupted sleep leaning on the cash register!

One day I finish moving the frequently moved bags and climb the stairs to the upper, main level. Uncle is red in the face with hot anger. A customer woke him up. Usually, he does not mind opening his eyes for a few minutes for a good sell. But Freddy Skiles has made him furious. Uncle allows people in the community to charge groceries and merchan-dise until pay-day. Sometimes, if a person gets one or two items, they don't even come to the cash register. The register sits on a homemade, u-shaped, counter where inside the "U" Uncle stands and often sleeps. These ghost-like shoppers come in the front door, head to an aisle, snatch bread or something, and stop at the door on the way out and say some-thing like, "I got a loaf of bread. Charge it!" Uncle pulls out a little seven by nine flip pad, finds the person's page, and writes down "loaf of bread."

When "pay-day" comes at the mill or the mine, folks drop in to cash their checks and pay their bills. Uncle's system, using the little "dun book," is the forerunner of Visa and MasterCard for sure.

Freddy Skiles seriously irritates Uncle that day. Freddy makes a quick stop, darts into the store to the dry goods section, and heads to the front door. He pauses at the door, holds up a man's wallet, and says, "Charge it!" When Freddy is out of sight, Uncle throws up his hands exclaiming, "Son of a gun! Why would anyone buy a wallet and charge it? Heavens, if he has to charge it, he doesn't have any money to put in it! I just don't understand some durn people."

One day, I finish moving the fifty pound bags early because I discover we are almost out of fifty pound horse feed. Before I move the one-hundred pound bags, I go tell Uncle he needs to order more fifty pound bags of horse feed. When I get upstairs, no one else is in the store, but Uncle is wide awake, with an aghast look on his face.

"Uncle, you okay? I ask

He says, "Yeah, but Paladin was just in here." Paladin was the main character in *Have Gun Will Travel*, a popular television western series in the 1950s.

"Uncle, what? what do you mean?" I mumble out.

Uncle says, "I guess I dozed off a little bit. I look up, and this man is standing right there." Pointing at the other side of the counter where customers stood. "I look at this man a minute because he doesn't say anything. So I just say to him, 'You look familiar, but I've never seen you around here.' And he just stands there. I say, 'You look just like that feller who plays Paladin on the tv.' The man sticks out his hand and says, 'I'm Richard Boone. We're over in Asheville working on a little filming project, and just thought I would drive over here this afternoon and see where my ancestors lived.'"

Uncle swears he met Paladin, Richard Boone, whose ancestors, sure enough, lived in the area. Squire Boone, Sr. had a slew of boys: Daniel Boone, Israel Boone (my direct ancestor), and several other boys including Squire Boone Jr. who was Richard Boone's direct ancestor. No one could verify Uncle's story, and it was so unbelievable I don't think he told hardly anyone else. I quickly forgot about the whole episode until now. Uncle said Richard Boone wanted to buy a pack of *Lucky Strikes*. Uncle said he just gave him the cigarettes and a pack of matches. Uncle isn't amused when a smart-aleck young teenager, says, "Put his name and a pack of cigarettes in that dun book, and maybe he'll come back on pay-day and pay us!"

Interestingly, Aaron Boone, manager of the New York Yankees and part of the Boone baseball-playing family with grandfather and brother all playing Major League Baseball, descended from Squire Boone, Sr. No one in Boonford claims seeing him or his MLB playing brother, Bret.

When one of the older residents of the area walks into Uncle's store and if another older resident happened to be in the store, they usually greet each other with, "Are you purt?" The other might respond with, "No, I'm kind of puny today." There are three possible responses to the question "Are you purt?" If you are feeling good, you say, "Yeah, I'm purt!" If you are not feeling too good, you say, "I'm kind of puny today" which means you're not 100%, maybe down with a cold or a bad back. The person might then ask Uncle for a pack of BC Powders, grab a Coke from the drink box, and after pouring the powder into the bottled drink, hoist up, and drink down the most common remedy for "puny." If you feel neither purt nor puny, you might offer to the interested person, "I'm fair to middlin" which means "mediocre" or "so-so." We never had a cure for that.

My first encounter with Raeford "Stingy" Smith is at my uncle's store. A thoroughly unique human being, Stingy always dresses, summer or winter, in a wool red plaid shirt, dirty gray "britches" that are too short for his six-foot/three-inch frame and do not reach his brown brogans, a stiff leather shoe reaching to the ankles. Apparently never been in a den-tist's chair, his teeth, the ones he still has, are as yellow as lemons. A full head of hair is gray like a confederate soldier's uniform. Unusually strik-ing, his behavior is the subject of much conversation around Boonford and Newdale. Stories about Stingy make their way from one household to another. His adventures are dinner time entertainment. He is known as "the stingiest man alive."

When I first work for Uncle, I notice Stingy approaching the store with a five-gallon red gas can. I figure he will purchase gas for his lawn-mower or garden tiller, but he sits quietly in front of the store on a bench that Uncle provides for those who want to "sit a spell" before going back to their homes and families. "Stingy" sits for about twenty minutes when Tish Blevins pulls her black two-door Ford Falcon to the gas pumps.

"Hello, Tish," I politely say as I walk up to her car. It was unheard of to pump your own gas in the 50s and 60s in this part of North Caro-lina. Gas was only fifteen cents per gallon, and every gas station has an employee, a youngster like me or a guy who couldn't get a job anywhere else, to pump gas for customers.

"How much you want?" I ask.

Tish, who always smelled like hairspray, scrambles through her over-sized red purse, "Oh, about a dollar's worth. I ain't been paid yet." (At fifteen cents per gallon that could be half of a tank.)

I pull the nozzle and hose off the regular pump but pause to say, "Regular, I guess?"

Still sorting in her pocketbook, "Yeah, that's fine and here's my money, thought maybe I lost it."

I finish pumping, return the nozzle and hose to the pump, take her four quarters, and head back into the store where I proudly announce to Uncle, "A dollar's worth of regular!" Turning around, full of pride and accomplishment, I see Stingy at the gas pump. He has taken the hose off the pump, has the nozzle in his gas can, and is shaking the hose vigorously.

"I guess Stingy's buying some gas," I note to Uncle, thinking I am supposed to do the pumping.

"He's getting gas all right, but he ain't buying," Uncle declares as he grimaces slightly but trying not to look too disapproving. "He just shakes what little is left in the hose into his red can. He'll be here most of the day shaking the hose out after each gas customer until he gets a half a gallon or so. I let him do it because his daddy and my daddy were good friends." My jaw drops, and I laugh.

Over the days ahead, I hear some interesting Stingy stories. His father was a Pentecostal preacher and brick layer who made Stingy read the Bible for four hours every day. Stingy developed a decidedly hated view of the church and his father to go along with a jaded view of the world. Once, he bought a new lawnmower but didn't want to buy the oil for the engine. He hung around the store for a couple of days and pulled several oil cans out of the garbage after motorists had stopped for a can of oil to top off their engines. He didn't get enough oil to bring the oil level in his engine up to the "add oil" level. By the end of that mowing season, his lawnmower engine "burnt up."

In the town of Burnsville, a new "all you can eat" buffet restaurant opens with fried chicken, steak, chicken livers, pork chops, and a wide assortment of vegetables and desserts. The restaurant owner develops a tremendous dislike for Stingy. The restaurant sits on a side-street in the little town. Stingy arrives late one Saturday evening, and the parking lot is full. He pulls as close as he can to the last car in the lot while leaving half of his car in the side street. It is not much of a problem since there is little traffic, other than the restaurant traffic. The street is a through-street, and the local sheriff comes into the restaurant about closing time and asks, "Who owns that red Mercury Comet with plastic taped over where the back window is supposed to be?" There are only three customers in the restaurant at this point, a couple paying at the cash register and Stingy. Stingy wipes his mouth with his shirt sleeve and confesses, "Officer, that would be mine. I'm going to get a new back window. Please don't give me a durn ticket."

"I'm not going to give you a ticket, but your car is parked half-way in the street. You'll need to move that right away." After all the other customers drive out of the parking lot, Stingy's red Comet sticks out like a red sore thumb into the street.

What most annoys the restaurant owner is how literally Stingy takes the "all you can eat" concept. He not only eats enough to feed a small family while he is in the restaurant, but the staff has to remind him constantly that he should not put chicken legs, pork chops, and various other foods from the buffet into his coat, shirt, and pants pockets to take home.

Too cheap to replace brakes on his car, Stingy tries to save wear and tear on the brake pads by rarely using his brakes. He lives about one-hundred yards off the main two-lane road. When he needs to go somewhere, he watches from his car as he sits in front of his house. His engine is running. When he sees no other car coming from the east, he starts toward the stop sign at the bottom of the slight incline where his road meets the main road. He doesn't want to use his brakes by stopping at the stop sign. He sees half of a mile up the road to the east but only sees about fifty yards to the west. A car can quickly come over the hill from the west. This intersection is not far from Uncle's store. Every few days, we hear horns blowing and tires screeching as Stingy goes through the intersection trying to beat a car that has come over the hill from the west. More than once, Uncle says, "Stingy is going to kill a week's burying one day."

One day, Stingy pulls out in front of another car, and a mild collision follows. Stingy's red Mercury Comet is dented up, but he does not want to tell his wife what happened and parks the car in their driveway with the dented side away from the house, so his wife cannot see the big dent. He makes an appointment with an insurance adjuster, but in a telephone call with the adjuster insists that he wants to meet in Burnsville in a grocery store parking lot. They agree to meet on a Friday morning at 10:00 AM. The adjuster arrives about five minutes early and waits in the parking lot.

He keeps looking for the red Comet, but it never arrives. He calls Stingy's house and explains to his wife that he is supposed to meet Stingy, but he has not seen a red Comet, reported being in the accident. She is surprised since Stingy has not told her about any of this.

Looking out the window of her house, Stingy's wife says, "Well, the red Comet is here, but our old truck is gone."

"What color is the truck?" The adjuster asks.

"Green, dark green," She says.

"Okay, I see it across the parking lot." The adjuster responds with puzzlement in his voice.

In his haste to conceal the damaged car from his wife, Stingy jumped in the wrong vehicle and sped away to meet the adjuster.

Sad stories circulate about what happens when Stingy's wife breaks her hip and is admitted to Spruce Pine hospital. Because he arrived early in the morning, the nurses are at first impressed by Stingy's devotion to his wife. A couple of nurses go into his wife's room after her breakfast tray arrives and notice that Stingy is helping himself to her breakfast. They politely asked him from then on to come after the breakfast hour.

Stingy continues to arrive just before the breakfast hour but goes to different floors of the hospital. At each nurses' station, he explains that his wife is on another floor, and he is politely waiting for her to finish her breakfast. The nurses on the other floors are flummoxed when Stingy inquires if anyone has "passed" during the night. At first, they think he is compassionate. What Stingy learned was that the kitchen staff rarely gets word of a patient's death during the night in time to cancel the break-fast tray's delivery to the deceased person's room. Since the body was removed overnight, Stingy, after making sure no one sees him, enters the room, and enjoys a hot breakfast.

Stingy's wife recovers enough to return home but is confined to bed. It is summertime, and the neighbors notice that the grass is only cut on about one-third of Stingy's lawn, and the remainder of the grass is almost knee-high. Stingy only cuts the grass that his wife can observe. Bed-ridden, she can only see out one window.

Stingy loves his brother William "Shaky" Smith. Shaky has an Es-sential Tremor, a neurological disorder causing involuntary shaking of the hands, limbs, and head. Many times in the store I assist Shaky in pulling dollar bills from his wallet.

One day, Shaky makes a purchase, and I ask, "How's your brother?"

"Don't know. I haven't seen him in a couple of weeks. He came by the house on my birthday with a card for me. I really appreciated it. After Stingy left, I turned the card over and the other side said, In Deepest Sympathy. My stingy brother was at a visitation at the funeral home the night before and picked up that sympathy card, flipped it over, and wrote Happy Birthday on the other side and gave it to me!" We enjoy a big laugh.

I miss out on one of the biggest events ever to happen in Uncle's store. Blue Rock is a community, named after a stunning blue rock that projects out of the side of a mountain. Blue Rock is not far from Boonford but separated by the ugly, polluted waters of the South Toe River. The river is not deep in some places, and sometimes people walk down the mountain and wade across the river to visit a friend in the opposite community. Rudy McCurry wades across the river one summer afternoon, and his foot hits a large object in the river. He reaches down and pulls out a Spanish Morion, a helmet worn by Spanish conquistadors led by Hernando de Soto who explored the North Carolina mountains in the sixteenth-century looking for gold. Rudy's first stop was Uncle's store. I was not working that day and missed the great find.

In the same area of Blue Rock where the Spanish Morion was found exists an ancient soapstone quarry hidden in the woods and known to very few. Dating to at least the Woodland Period (1000 BC), Native American carvers of the Mississippian Culture chiseled and lifted large bowls out of the soft soapstone-rock faces on a ridge just above the river. Were the Spanish soldiers, who lost a helmet (a soldier?) in the river, searching for the quarry? Maybe best for them if they did not find it. My grandfather warned me to stay away because of asbestos in the soapstone, saying that the ancient bowl excavators might have become sick and died from asbestos exposure.

Murdocks and the Holy Night

*"Our greatest enemies, the ones we
must fight most often, are within . . ."*

THOMAS PAINE

ALL THE LOCALS COME by Uncle's store, including the Murdocks. Cole
Murdock and his brother Creed are so mean they even play tricks on
the local law enforcement. They "pay" the sheriff, commonly called the
sheriff's relief fund, to look the other way as they engage in the illegal
retail trade of bootlegging. Incredibly, they still harass the sheriff and
his deputies.

One hot summer night, Cole and Creed spot one of the local deputies, Curl Griffin, parked up a small dirt road that intersects with the
Boonford road. For no reason except to get a big laugh, Creed in the
darkness quietly crawls under the rear of the deputy's car and carefully
slips a logging chain around the rear axle. Securing one end to the axle,
he crawls out and without being noticed secures the other end of the
chain around a big oak tree. Creed makes his way through the darkness
to where Cole, in the red Charger, is sitting around the curve. With Creed
aboard, Cole heads up the road, gaining speed quickly. They are at high,
illegal speed when they go past the deputy's car. Creed holds up a middle
finger as they streak by the deputy.

The deputy is instantly enraged! Speeding and giving him the finger! They'll pay for this! He grabs the gear shift lever, dropping the car
into drive. His foot quickly pushes the gas pedal to the floor. The engine
roars, the car bolts forward, and is on track to chase down the Murdocks.
Suddenly, the car abruptly stops with a tremendous jerk backward. The

deputy is propelled forward, and his head slams into the steering wheel. Blood is everywhere as he sees stars, little specks of light, as he battles to stay conscious. He is aware enough to see the red Charger in reverse backing down the road. The red Charger pulls alongside the deputy's car. In the passenger seat of the Murdock mobile, Creed snickers as he says, "Looks like your car needs some training, stopped in mid-flight on you!" Cole and Creed roar with laughter as they pull away. A few years earlier, Curl Griffin and Cole Murdock were friends and played pool together. A mountain proverb says, "Just because you feed the wolf today, doesn't mean he won't eat you tomorrow."

The bootlegging enterprise yields big profits, and challengers often arise for the Murdocks. The economy is perpetually weak in the mountains. The Great Depression never ended. Good jobs are hard to find. Local factories have waiting lists for even the lowest-paying positions. Some folks are lucky and secure jobs in far-away places like Asheville or Marion, but the cost of driving takes a big slice out of the paychecks.

Driven by economic scarcity and youthful ambition, another rival enters the illicit booze market. When in school, Lenny Fox is a nightmare for every teacher. He does not do his work, challenges the teachers' authority, and mocks the teachers openly, which usually gets him sent to the office. The principal, James England, can't handle him either. At least once a week, Lenny gets a thunderous paddling in the principal's office, and Lenny always emerges with the claim, "He can't hurt me!" There was great relief among the teachers when Lenny drops out of school in the tenth grade.

Like Lenny challenges the teachers, in a couple of years, he takes on the Murdocks, indirectly at first. Lenny starts selling his secondhand beer and liquor out of his car, outside the local pool hall. Lenny even has assistants. Barnum and Bailey Higgins (their mother loved the circus) can't find work either.

"No one will put us on." They tell Lenny. "We'll help you. Murdocks don't scare us none."

Lenny's parents long ago kicked him out of the house. For a while no one knows where he is living. Word circulates Lenny lives with his dementia-inflicted grandmother. He brings along aide de camps, Barnum and Bailey, plus Everett "Lightning" Wilson. Everett is called Lightning because as a little boy he urinated on a live electric fence, designed to stop a bull with the legal limit of 10,000 volts. Everybody calls him "Lightning" except for some of the other younger boys. They call him

"Crazy Cod" because they have seen the deformity caused by the high voltage. They tease Everett, "Your girlfriends will find you electrifying!" And they crackle with laughter. These partners in crime call themselves "The Arbuckle Boys," naming themselves after Arbuckle Road that intersects with Highway 80 in Boonford. Apparently, they did not know that an "Arbuckle" was "a dupe," "gullible person," or "a stooge."

It's like a fraternity house at grandma's place at the end of the dirt road. Lenny's grandmother says, "They are such nice boys." Sadly sometimes she mistakes one of them for her son killed in the war. With the memory reducing dementia, Granny can't keep up with the number of visitors that come to see Lenny and his friends at her house. These visitors are not making social calls. The news circulates that Lenny's booze is less expensive than the inflated prices long charged by the Murdocks. The Murdocks fear no man, not even Lenny. When they start hearing "talk" about their new rival, the Murdocks hatch a plan.

The Murdocks think Christmas Eve a perfect time to ambush their latest rival Lenny and his circus boys, as Cole calls them. Cole and Creed will wait for them at the intersection of Arbuckle Road and Highway 80. Lenny has a reputation as a fierce fighter, but the Murdocks think they can take Lenny and the circus boys. A good beating will curtail their interest in their "retail trade." Word gets to the Murdocks that Lenny knows of the ambush and is holed up just up the road in Burl Bishop's barn. Clever fellows, the Murdocks decide to set the barn on fire and then "engage" Lenny and the circus boys as they flee the fire.

The Murdocks make two miscalculations: Lenny is in Bill Tipton's barn, not Burl Bishop's. And the local people hate Burl's barn, old and dilapidated, a real eyesore.

The barn stands across the road from Born Again Church where the faithful are gathered for the annual Christmas Eve service. Pastor Leroy concludes his sermon, which is always about the perils of going to Hell (and many souls are going to Hell, rich Episcopalians, Gandhi, Buddhist monks, anyone who was not born-again), when Effie Penland spots the barn flames.

Folks in the community call Effie an "old maid," but apparently she was a beauty in her early days. She still has eyes as blue as the Mediterranean. The reason she is single is probably due to her involuntary and frequent burps that startle strangers but are a familiar sound to all of us.

"Burl's barn burning!" she screams as Pastor Leroy is about to give the altar call. Burl and family sit near the back and are the first ones out the door when Effie sounds the alarm. Everyone else figures they better go lend a hand. So the whole congregation goes across the road, but it is too late. Flames engulf the structure but not a tear is shed. Burl even remarks "time that old barn came down."

Effie believes she has a great singing voice, but everyone talks about how she "hollers" when she sings. At that moment with the entire congregation standing in front of the burning barn, Effie breaks into "O Holy Night," and everyone joins in, as much to cover up Effie's hollering as anything.

Word quickly spreads through the community that Burl's old barn is on fire. Soon gathered in front of the flames is every resident of Boonford, all singing Christmas carol after Christmas carol. Standing there are some of the Murdock's best customers, folks who have not been to church in years like the Howells, yes, even those Pastor Leroy declared were "going to Hell."

On the ridge above the church on the Arbuckle Road, the Murdocks gather in their cars, watching the impromptu festival below. Cole and Creed are in one car, and one-armed Lester and his wife in another. They are hoping to watch the beating that Cole and Creed will put on Lenny but have been told by Cole that their prey has escaped. The moonlight glistens off Cole's chrome wheels. Lenny and his boys will not be beaten this night, but Cole will be soon plotting his revenge.

But for this night, this Holy Night, the good people, saved and unsaved, of Boonford stood arm in arm, a Christmas glow on their faces, and the joy of Christmas in their hearts. Lenny, Lightning, Barnum, and Bailey pull up and join the crowd, not out of reverence, but out of curiosity and for a hostile gesture toward the Murdocks.

Ironically, the Murdocks give us the best Christmas ever! The entire community gathers together as no one could have dreamed. Effie has a nephew, Moe, almost eighteen, who has not uttered a word in his life, but always has an incredibly big smile on his face. "Elective mute," the parents say the doctors have told them. Effie swears that night standing in front of the barn bonfire she hears Moe whisper "Christmas."

Tragedy marks Effie's life. Students made fun of her at school because of the burping. She drops out to work as a caretaker for an elderly bedridden Mr. Grindstaff in his home. The pay is not much but at least something. She can't expect much as a drop-out. Mr. Grindstaff has a grandson, Phil, who has his own acute emotional problems. Phil has Tourette's Syndrome and involuntarily shrieks, screeches, and barks. It seems to happen when he is anxious.

Phil visits his aging grandfather from time to time. Phil and eyes have met a few times during his visits. One evening, Effie follc Phil out to the porch. A stormy evening, rain pelts the ground beyond the porch and lightning streaks across the sky. They talk for what seems like hours and say goodnight. A few days later Phil returns, and once again, they talk. Both feel a connection and energy like they have never felt before. The full moon rises above the mountain as they look at each other's lips. Heads go forward and then their lips meet. Neither Effie nor Phil thought they would ever find their soul mates, with the burping and barking, but here they are together, giggly happy.

The relationship blossoms and flourishes. Phil is a truck driver, drives an eighteen-wheeler, and hauls logs down the mountain to the hardwood sawmill near Marion. He knows better, but going down the steep, winding road from Spruce Pine to Marion, he does not gear down but instead rides his brakes. His brakes overheat, and he cannot stop the loaded truck at the bottom of the mountain. He has too much speed, runs off the road, and crashes into a dry creek bed. The big trailer on the back jack-knifes. Chains don't hold, and logs flip through the air. One large log crushes the cab. The love of Effie's life vanishes in death.

Fraught Search for Acceptance

*"Youth is the most precious thing in life;
it is too bad it has to be wasted on young folks."*

GEORGE BERNARD SHAW

BOONFORD. FRIENDLY? HOSTILE? TERRIFYING? Boonford excelled in all. By mountain standards, I had a good family. My mother is loving and supportive, but the surrounding area could be lawless and like a war zone. One Saturday morning, we are taking the weekly Saturday morning trip to town, Spruce Pine, about fifteen miles away. It is an essential trip every Saturday. At the time, it is the only place to get groceries, a haircut, or pick up something from a hardware store. There were a couple of exceptions. Long before Amazon starts making home deliveries, Robinson's Dairy leaves glass quart jars of fresh milk on our front porch three times per week. Sad is the day we are told that home milk delivery is a thing of the past, never to be seen again. So we get our milk on the Saturday run "to town." Basically, everyone from the surrounding countryside is there, walking the streets, upper and lower of the little town since it is built on the side of a mountain.

On the way this Saturday morning, we round a curve and in front of us is a marital brawl of epic proportions. Homer and Ginger do not own a car but ride every Saturday morning with a friend to the Spruce Pine stores. On the return trip, they are let out on the side of the road near their house and are having a disagreement that has turned into a slugfest but only after they have each thrown everything in their grocery bags at each other. Broken jars and bottles, cans, cereal boxes litter the highway. Interestingly, Ginger, a large and athletic woman, is now winning. Homer is in "rope a dope" (a defensive position that Muhammad Ali would later make famous). Ginger lunges at Homer and takes him down. They roll down a bank and into a creek. Their clothes are soaked, and their hair hangs down in their faces, as they climb up the bank. Fortunately, it is summer. They do not get hypothermia, but they will miss a few meals that week with their groceries splattered in the road.

I attend school with Homer and Ginger's son, "Chase." Chase is not Richard's real name. Homer nicknamed him "Chase." Homer is unemployed most of his life and spends most of his afternoons drinking Pabst Blue Ribbon in the can. Their mobile home is on the side of a mountain with a steep slope descending into the woods about fifty yards away. Chase told me that his father starts drinking about the time he gets home from school each day. Homer sits in a folding chair in from of the mobile home. After finishing each beer, he gives the empty can a toss down the slope. Chase and his sister, Abby, run down the slope in a race to secure the empty beer can and bring it back up the hill. Abby is faster than Richard and almost always gets to the beer can first. One day, Homer declares, "Richard, I am going to call you Chase because you are always chasing your sister."

A bright young man, Chase earns a full scholarship to Emory University in Atlanta. Homer and Ginger travel to see him for parents' weekend. The roommate's parents from New York are also visiting. They all arrive on Friday evening staying at Chase's apartment because they have an extra bedroom and a sofa that makes into a bed. Ginger very determined to impress the roommates' parents tries to sound like she is not from the mountains. With the boys still sleep the next morning, all the adults gather in the kitchen to sip hot coffee except Homer. Back home, Ginger always fixes Homer a breakfast of eggs and bacon. Homer comes into the apartment kitchen, points to a dozen eggs on the counter, and says to Ginger (as he would do back home in the mountains), "Ginger, fix me some auggs." Like a lot of mountain folk, 'auggs' is the way Homer says eggs. Ginger trying not to look embarrassed responds, "Homer, they are not auggs." Homer runs his fingers through his uncombed matted hair and fires back, "Well, if they ain't auggs, what in the hell are they then?"

Chase and I join the Boy Scouts together. Excited, we get our uniforms and camping equipment. The mess kits and canteens are so cool. After receiving our Tenderfoot badge, we are allowed to go on our first troop camping trip. I've never been camping before. A van takes us to a trailhead, and we hike a trail deep into the forest to a campsite. So thrilled, we put up our tents, roll out our sleeping bags, and help the scoutmaster prepare dinner. We have a gourmet meal of hot dogs on a stick grilled over an open fire. The scoutmaster, Mr. Bryant, is about fifty years old with a son in the troop. Mr. Bryant likes to stroke the dark whiskers on his chin, wears black horned rimmed glasses, and enjoys sharing his scientific knowledge with us. We listen to an evening science lesson for we are all working on our science badges.

The evening campfire illuminates a wide circle around the fire. We sit on rocks and large pieces of wood, and listen to the fire crackle and pop. Embers drift into the night sky. Mr. Bryant tells us we are in for a surprise. Roasted marshmallows along with chocolate will be placed between graham crackers for tasty bedtime treats. But first Mr. Bryant announces he needs two volunteers. He has gone into the woods and brought back several pieces of root. The root is a little known but delicious delicacy, he tells us. He only has enough for two boys. Chase and I shoot our hands into the air. Mr. Bryant invites us to come around the fire to where he sits for our special surprise. I have been assertive and get one of the root treats. I am proud of myself.

At first the root seems interesting as I chew. I wait for a pleasing flavor, maybe sweet, to wash across my tongue and the inside of my mouth. Soon, I realize something is wrong. A stinging sensation starts on my tongue and spreads to the inside of my cheeks. Alarmed, I look at Mr. Bryant. A snickering smile sweeps across his face. His son starts to laugh. The other boys point fingers at us and roar with laughter. My mouth sears with hot pain. Mr. Bryant tricked and deceived us. The root is not edible. It is a backwoods prank to pull on the unsuspecting. We were trusting, and he took advantage of us. My mouth is on fire with pain all night long. Water does not help. Nothing helps. I crawl into my sleeping bag with tears of misery running down my cheeks. Mr. Bryant has violated all the Boy Scout oaths to be loyal and trustworthy to have a laugh at our expense. My mouth burns with hot scorching sensations, but the rest of my being burns with anger at that man. Will I ever trust an authority figure again?

Boonford wept with loneliness for kids. An elderly couple lives in the old white house across the road for the first few years of my life. Every summer, their daughter from Florida visits for a week, bringing her husband and children. We play all day and into the night until our parents make us go to bed. "Old man kick the can" and "hide and seek" are our favorite games. I love that week! But it is a crushing sadness when they leave. No one to play with until next summer. The elderly couple die in a few years, and my playmates stop coming.

Years later as a young teenager, I work in Uncle's grocery store carrying out groceries, pumping gas, stocking shelves. Into the store walks the family, making a long overdue visit to the area. "David, do you remember me?" says Rachel, "I use to play Old Man Kick The Can with you." She is now "drop-dead gorgeous" with long dark hair, deep brown eyes, and the figure of a Hollywood actress. I fall in love for the first time.

Rachel and her family come "from off somewhere", not a term of endearment when said by mountain people about others. Mountain folks, particularly then, view suspiciously anyone who has not grown up in the area. My mother warned me "if you go off to college someday, you'll end up being from off somewhere" and that would not be good. The summer people from Florida are from off somewhere, but they keep to themselves (intentionally away from us) in the exclusive resorts on tops of mountains. Florida families send their children to summer camps in the mountains. As one young woman from the sunshine state about my age of sixteen at the time said, "My father is a dermatologist. He sends me here to keep me off the beaches. He thinks I won't get skin cancer here." Ski resorts like Beech Mountain, Hound Ears, Sugar Mountain are not far away. But only people from off somewhere go there. We laugh at them because we can't understand why anyone wants to go to the top of a mountain to freeze and fall down in the snow. Most of the local men work outside all week long in the mines and forests, and the last thing they want is to be outside.

Certain behaviors make a person from off somewhere easy to spot by the locals. On the highway, when the locals pass each other, they "throw up their hand" as a friendly greeting. You could also raise the index finger of the hand on the steering wheel or even raise the chin and throwback the head as a greeting. If the driver of the passing car did not throw up the hand, raise the finger, or throw back the head, they were certainly from off somewhere and to be viewed with great suspicion.

A family from off somewhere moves here from Florida. They buy an old farm, back at the end of a "holler" (the way we say hollow). They have two Mercedes cars, unheard of to have one, let alone two. The attractive couple has two teenage children that are home-schooled (an alien concept in those days . . . some kids do not go to school but they are not "schooled" at home . . . never learn to read and write unless they teach themselves). The glamorous family comes to the grocery store where I work as a teenager. It is always a sweeping, stunning entrance. The wife is dressed like she just walked out of Frederick's of Hollywood and always showing an abundance of cleavage, with lots of fatty tissue in all the right places.

Soon, the man from off somewhere starts a business of going door to door and offering to install "water softeners" because he claims the mountain water is "so hard it ruins your pipes and makes you sick." The water test is free, but every test results in the need for a water softener. He has a partnership with a local mechanic to install the water treatment systems. They sell lots of them until the local high school science teacher takes water samples to a state lab. He discovers the natural water in peoples' wells is already soft and safe to use. People who had bought the treatment systems are outraged and demand their money back. One man goes to their house to get his money and returns saying that the entire family was naked, walking around outside, mother, father, and teenagers. "Nudists! We have nudists from Florida living here!" It's a terrible thing. God's judgment might be visited on the entire community. Shunned and scorned, the family soon leave the area but not after a few men go to their house demanding refunds or innocently explaining they are lost and need directions! Our prejudice against people from off somewhere is hardened for sure.

"Communists" move to the area from New York and (in the locals' view) other God-forbidden places. To this day, the area attracts artists, potters, and other artisans. In my childhood, these people from off somewhere keep to themselves in little communities with their own schools, community associations, and artist communities. The men have long hair and beards (we had not yet heard of hippies). The women are scantily clad even when in their organic vegetable gardens. They swim nude in river swimming holes, and unsuspecting local canoes float by within a few feet of female bare-breasted river bathers. They are not Soviet-style communists or anything like that. They are highly educated intellectuals and artists who loved nature and the mountain environment and want to raise their children in like-minded communities. In my early lonely teenage years, I long to socialize with teenagers from these communities, but I can't bridge the cultural gap, except for an occasional romantic episode that is always short-lived.

My older brother and sister live the first few years of their lives without electricity. In the evenings, they only have the dim light of candles. When the electricity comes on for the first time, the bulbs first flicker and then shine brightly. They jump up and down with excitement for they have never seen such bright luminance. My brother and sister are part of the "out-house generation." When I come along, fortunately, we have bathrooms, but we still get our water from a spring, further up the mountain. The "spring house" is a cinderblock building about five feet tall with its own roof and about the size of a Volkswagon Beetle. Green moss grows up the cinder blocks and over the roof. A pipe sticks out through one of the cinder blocks on the bottom row. A pipe carries our water by gravity down to our house. When I want to go fishing in the North Toe River, I go up to the spring house. I can push the top back enough to see inside. In the pool of water, bubbling up from the rocks below, I always find some fine orange or black lizards for fishing. Probably a good thing, I don't think about the lizards when I have a glass of our drinking water.

My brother and sister are born at home. Is there a midwife? I don't know. I am born in the Marion hospital about forty-five minutes away. My sister wants a baby sister in the worse kind of way. The story goes that after I am born and before I come home, my mother explains to my sister that she is getting a baby brother and not a baby sister. My mother is "quick on her feet." When she sees the disappointment on Carolyn's face, she explains, "I know you want a little sister but the only little girls they have here to choose from are from other countries and none of them look like us. Is it okay if we take a little boy home that looks like us?" Begrudgingly, my sister agrees, and she brings home a little brother. She teases me to this day that she dressed me like a little girl when my mother wasn't looking. Luckily I escape a gender identity disorder.

I painfully remember the intense loneliness when my brother and sister go to college when I am a little boy. Sometimes, they come home for the weekend, bringing fun and laughter with them. But then we drive them back to college on Sunday and drive back home late on Sunday evening in the dark. I sit in the back of the car in the darkness and all by myself. Again, we have no neighbors, no children to play with. So I invent my own friends. Out back in a dirt pile, I establish an imaginary trucking company. I am the boss, and Junior, Tackhead, and Bobby (names I adopt from local men) are my main drivers. I get a football suit for Christmas and have great games in the front yard. I play for the Green Bay Packers and take turns being Paul Horning, Jim Ringo, or Bart Starr. I fall down when an imaginary Philadelphia Eagle makes a good tackle. If not, I streak down an imaginary sideline for a touchdown. My father doesn't have the energy for me. He is an older parent and works at manual labor all day. He is exhausted when he gets home. For indoor entertainment, I take marbles and a big piece of cardboard (cutting holes in the cardboard). If the marble falls into the hole it is an "out" and if not it is a "hit." I have a major league baseball organization. I get my hands on some "baseball" cards (that come with packs of bubble gum) with pictures of players like Willie Mays and Mickey Mantle and those are my rosters.

Almost every adult male in the community receives a nickname, especially if a person has any kind of body abnormality. Is it a way for people to entertain themselves? Sometimes, nicknaming is cruel. Pothead, not so named because he rolled joints, his head is naturally shaped like a pot. I don't know if it was the methods of giving birth, but some men have funny shaped heads and lend themselves to nicknames. Churnhead is another one (a churn is a large oblong jar that was used to separate butter from milk). Flathead and Saucerhead are other names. A man is nicknamed Auger Eye Ellis. It would have been too hard calling him Nystagmus Eye Ellis, a rare disorder where the eyeball involuntarily rotates when the head is turned in certain positions. Interestingly, he has two younger brothers whose eyeballs also rotate when their heads turn in the same positions, although the doctors say they don't have nystagmus. Consciously or unconsciously, they want to be like big brother.

An industrious fellow, Tackhead develops a profitable hobby. He lives in a mobile home on a small farm he inherits from his deceased parents that sits just off Highway 80. Like many mobile home sites, a bull-dozer has cut out a small section of flat earth from the side of the mountain where the mobile home resides. A small driveway and a tiny yard are also mauled out of the side of the mountain. Tackhead does not use the pasture land beside his house. He allows car repair shops and wrecker services to bring their undrivable and unrepairable cars and drop them on the inclined field. Over the years, he has collected rows and rows of wrecked cars that now form a massive car graveyard on what was once a beautiful pastoral scene on the side of the mountain. For one dollar, customers can make their way through the auto-graveyard pulling off parts for needed repairs. The field of dead cars and trucks displaying every make, model, and color, most with hoods up, bumpers missing, doors open, and front windshields shattered, jolts the drivers and passengers on the highway as they pass by, particularly those seeing the field of mangled metal and the kaleidoscope colors for the first time. A local man with environmental concerns dubs the car graveyard "The Field of Shame", a tragic depository for the waste of the industrial age.

The Field of Shame becomes the quick and final resting place for Yancey County's only Thing. Tackhead in addition to inheriting the farm also inherited a "small piece of money." In Asheville, a slick-talking car salesman convinced Tackhead he must own the first Thing. Volkswagon manufactured the Thing and imported them to the US. The Thing was described by a car magazine as "the illegitimate love-child of a corrugated shipping container and a dumpster." Although boxy, flimsy, and comical, Tackhead turned heads as he drove through the streets of Burnsville and Spruce Pine in his Thing. His narcissistic glory is short-lived however. Ralph Nader led a consumer safety push that causes the Thing to be condemned and ordered off the highways for failing to meet basic safety standards. Tackhead's Thing became the laughable novelty of The Field of Shame.[3]

Before I start school, I walk down the bank from our house and wait with my brother and sister for the morning school bus. Every morning all eyes look out for the "The Flying Woman." A professional living on the other side of Boonford headed to an office job in one of the little towns. About 7:45 AM when I see her down the road, I exclaim, "Here she comes! Here comes The Flying Woman!" Her car disappears behind a big curve carved out on the side of the mountain. Suddenly, her car reappears in front of us and goes roaring by at a high rate of speed, as we cheer and wave. My mother makes sure we move back from the road because The Flying Woman truly flies up the road, well beyond posted speed limits. She is often distracted as she puts on lipstick or combs her hair, making her even more dangerous, as her heavy foot is on the gas pedal.

Once a year, The Flying Woman deceives us. Before we recognize her familiar car coming up the road she goes roaring by in a new car. Her cars are always new "muscle cars," large cars with big engines and loud exhausts, a contrast to our family car. Every ten to fifteen years, my parents save up enough to buy a car. They keep the car until it is undrivable. We get a lot of snow and a lot of snow melting salt on the mountain roads. The salt over time causes the metal on the underside of cars to rust. Usually, that is not a problem for folks as they "trade cars" every few years. My father keeps his cars so long that the rust causes huge holes in the lower sections of our cars. A fellow worker, Pappy Price, teases my father, "Yep, you know it is Jack Howell's car coming down the road. You can see his leg hanging out!" I get to know this fellow worker by working at the mine over the summer and Christmas breaks while in college.

Pappy cannot read or write but has one of the quickest wits I ever witness. He has the build, head shape, and hair of Junior Samples a star on *Hew Haw*, the famed country music and comedy television show of years past. Except, Pappy has striking blond hair and brilliant blue eyes, no doubt a descendant of Scotch-Irish settlers who fled the Anglican persecution in England, a couple of centuries earlier. My father tells us that Pappy considers himself an amateur scientist although he has never gone to school. When the astronauts first go to the moon, my father comes home from work and shares with us that Pappy declares it a hoax. My father asks Pappy how he knows it is a hoax? According to my father, Pappy declares, "if they are really on the moon, they would not have to blast off. They would just let go because as you can tell from looking up at the moon at night it is downhill from the moon to the earth!" Citizen science has its place.

I soon bore of being the lookout for The Flying Woman. I have worn the rubber off my tricycle tires, riding all day up and down the sidewalk that stretches from the top of our bank to our front steps. I am intensely lonely spending all those days by myself. My mother and I go on "field trips" occasionally. These are not field trips to museums or historical sites. Literally, we go to my uncle's bean or cabbage "field" and pick vegetables. We work for hire sometimes and sometimes for our own consumption. But that is not what I want to do all day, having the hot sun beating down on me doing the back breaking work. After a day of picking for our own purposes, the next day we go to a friend's house to use her canning kitchen, an outdoor facility with a stove and tables. Cabbage is boiled and then packed in Mason jars with salt so that in the coming winter we have pickled cabbage (sauerkraut).

I don't want to be a farmer though or even a food processor. So I demand to go to school. Kindergarten does not exist. School starts with first grade. Problem is, I am only four years old, but I am so incredibly lonely and bored. The boredom soon ends. I go to school.

I still remember the "fits." My mother called them. Today, they are called "temper tantrums" or "anger episodes." I felt "rage" for I knew it was the only way to get my way. School has already started when my mother could stand "the fits" no more. She drives me to Micaville School. First through twelfth grades are in one large, gray stone building in Micaville, NC. There are four of these schools in the county, and each educates young boys and girls for twelve years in the same building. Each building has twelve rooms, one for each grade level.

The first-grade teacher, Mrs. Justice, says to my mother, "No problem. He's ain't too young." Indeed, no age restrictions for school attendance exist in Yancey County then. Parents put you in school when they want to, and if they don't want to, that is okay as well. No standards. No laws. So once I was four years old and proudly in the first-grade with new dungarees (jeans) and a plaid shirt. My hairstyle is a "flat-top." Hair is short and perfectly even, but the front is slightly longer, held upright with Lucky Tiger Cru-Butch Control Wax. My school-mates are not of uniform age. Boys, twelve years old, are finally starting first grade. They look odd in those little desks, barely squeezing into them, their legs wrapping around the desks in front of them.

Ramps and Reconciliation

"Patience is bitter but its fruit is sweet."
ARISTOTLE

I LOVE SCHOOL, LEARNING, and my classmates. Four years old and immature, I don't want to use the nasty bathrooms. I go to urinate, but I am not sitting on those nasty toilet seats. That is not a problem until one fateful day.

It's back to school after Christmas break. I have new dungarees again and now cowboy boots. Proud of these cowboy boots, they come up almost to my knees. My jeans tuck down into my boots, so I can show off these boots of renown. This little dude has style.

I don't sense an urgent problem that day until about an hour before the dismissal bell. A bubbling sensation brews for several hours in my stomach. At this hour before dismissal, I need urgently to go to the bathroom. Stubbornly, I am not sitting on those filthy seats that are out in the open in the boys' bathroom, no privacy whatsoever. So I am determined to wait until I get home.

The bell rings, and we all head to the buses. Just short of the bus, it happens. I can't hold it any longer. I am overpowered by my own bowels. "Oh no, it is in the seat of pants." I try to hold more back. I cannot. It is diarrhea, running down my leg, soon both legs, and into my boots. The boots are squishy as I approach the bus. I stand in line, waiting my turn to climb up the steps into the bus. The excrement keeps coming. "Maybe my boots will not overflow" and "if I don't say anything, maybe no one notices" is my hope.

I try to make my way to the back of the bus, but you can't fool kids, like you can't hold diarrhea but so long. They smell it, and at first hushed giggles greet me. They look at me in disbelief. Some hold their noses. Laughter starts to roar up and down the rows of seats. The bus driver, before departing and hearing the laughter, figures out what is going on. He comes to the back of the bus and encourages the other students to move forward. It is humiliation. I am all alone with my boots and my poop. But it gets worse when the bus stops in front of my house. I have to walk to the front of the bus, but I rather walk to the gallows. It is a gauntlet of laughter and humiliation. Jeers and taunts greet me as I pass each set of seats to the right and left. I hold back tears until I get off the bus. Then, as my bowels had emptied, so do my emotions. My mother is there, waiting for me, as she always was during that first year of school (she goes back to work soon in the factory). She helps me get undressed and cleaned up. The day of humiliation is nearly unbearable. But life goes on, and school goes on. In the days ahead, the students turn their attention to some other miserable kid of the day. It is amazing how cruel kids can be.

Academically, I enjoy school. If I study, it is easy. I have underlying insecurity that motivates me. I don't want to be found lacking or insufficient. An experience in the third grade haunts me for several years. In class during art time, the teacher dims the lights and then invites each child to come forward and sit in front of a bright light that results in a silhouette, an image, of each child's head on the wall. A black and white sketch is made of each child's head, and, later, we are asked to tape our "heads" on the hall wall outside our classroom for all to see. My head looks abnormal, too big, I am convinced. I decide I am deformed and kindly no one has told me. The kid with the enlarged head, I am. I imagine other kids laughing behind my back as I walk the halls.

Eventually, I move on to other concerns. A student is diagnosed with leukemia. We are told that she bleeds from her nose and eyes. My imagination works overtime. I am confident I will have leukemia in a matter of weeks, if not days. The young girl dies, a harsh reality for her classmates. Another classmate has meningitis. My neck hurts. Fortunately, he recovers and so do I from the somatic symptom.

Dreaded ramps appear in the spring. Ramps, a wild onion, grow at high elevations under a shady canopy of beech, sugar maple, poplar, or birch trees. They are sometimes called the first greens of spring. Folks in the mountains might have gone all winter without fresh vegetables. My forager mother finds (instead of ramps) "creasy greens," the real first greens, in late winter, poking up through the snow. Barbaraea verna is now called "upland cress" or "winter cress." My mother's "creasy greens" are now a valued commodity among the grow your own, eat healthy, population, but growing wild they saved us from scurvy at winter's last moment.

The schools fear the day each spring when allium tricoccum starts pushing up out of the ground. The wild ramps eaten in the mountains are much stronger than the ramps (wild leeks) grown on farms today and served as a garnish on pricey dishes at fashionable restaurants in major cities. Back then, the saying was "eat ramps raw in the spring and people will smell them on your breath in the fall." The pungent plant was not as odiferous when cooked. Many are still scrambled with eggs and added to a side of streaked meat and fresh-baked biscuits for a hardy mountain breakfast.

Years ago, before video games and electronics, boys living high in the mountains had to entertain themselves some way. In early spring, Clyde McIntosh, whose family lived higher up on the mountain than any other family in the area, would eat the first harvest. Raw! The next day and every day for the next couple of weeks until the ramps flowered and matured Clyde comes to school with an unbearable odor that is not only on his breath but radiating out of every pore of his skin. The odor would probably send rotting-flesh eating buzzards gagging and flying away. Fortunately, he is the only kid in our class who ate ramps raw. He must have had one of the original "raw bars" in his house, but they were not serving oysters. On the first day following Clyde's ramp feast, the classroom is re-arranged. No matter how cold it is outside, windows are fully opened. We are instructed to push our desks to the far right side of the room until we can barely squeeze between desks. We help the teacher push her big heavy, wooden desk to the far right corner of the room as well. Clyde might as well be a leper during ramp season because he has to put his desk to the far left of the classroom. And there he sits, all by himself, for several weeks. I felt sorry for Clyde and ask my mother if I could invite him over to play.

Clyde's father and mother do pay a visit to the principal's office the first time Clyde gets ostracized. Clyde's mother, pathologically shy, rarely speaks. Her hair speaks for her. Brilliant red, they call her Lil' Red. She is a common-law wife. Occasionally, she is seen from the valley below, standing on Bear Cave Ridge, her red hair glowing in the sunlight. Barron McKinney swore he saw her naked standing on the ridge, her arms lifted, and palms toward the heavens.

Big Junior McIntosh, Clyde's father, logs. They call him Big Junior for two reasons. He is a big man, and he had a little brother, a stepbrother, also called Junior. So little brother becomes Little Junior. Big Junior works the highest ridges for the local timber company. Not many people want the job. It is dangerous work with steep ridges and cliffs. He harvests tall, straight, virgin timber that stands on the mountain tops. Since motorized logging vehicles, like John Deere skidders, have no road up to the summit, Junior skids the logs down the mountain using a mule. Word is that Junior made his boss a wealthy man bringing down a bountiful walnut tree crop. Junior's boss rewards him with a truck, a brand spanking new truck with the biggest wheels and tires anyone in the mountains has ever seen, a rugged beauty.

Shortly after Junior takes possession of his new truck, he drives into Burnsville late one afternoon with a dead "eight-foot" timber-rattlesnake secured with a rope and stretched across the hood of his truck. Mature timber-rattlesnakes grow to six feet in length, but Junior has brought in a monster. A huge crowd gathers in front of the Nu Wray Inn. They stare at the behemoth snake and then at the bright and shining truck "the likes of which they have never seen."

In the truck of renown, Big Junior McIntosh and Lil' Red pull into the parking lot of Micaville Elementary School. He steps out of the truck and spits a big loogie on the asphalt parking lot. "I desire to see the principal," he tells the secretary in his thunderous voice. The secretary says, "Go on back and sit in his office til he gets back in thar. Principal England also teaches eighth grade, you know, but they are bout to go out to recess."

Big Junior down off the mountain top after over a half-day of logging has not changed his clothes. Everyone says Junior is a great mechanic. Evidence of mechanical difficulties is on his clothes as they are spattered with dark grease, smudges on his face, the part of his face that can be seen. Big Junior has not shaved in years. He would make John Godwin and Jay Stone of *Duck Dynasty* ashamed of their wimpy beards. Lil' Red puts a cooking pot over Big Junior's head every few months and trims his hair. I heard my mother say, after seeing him in the grocery store, "that's the woolliest man I've ever seen!" Big Junior, a hulking man, could easily play the part of a fierce Viking in the "picture shows."

With boots caked in mud and grease from his clothes already on the principal's fine cloth chair that the faculty gave him for Christmas, Big Junior waits. Principal England is a short, balding man in his early sixties who is counting the days to retirement. Principal has a round face and jaws that hang down. The students call him "Bull Dog." His son is in the fifth grade, and they call him "Pup." His wife teaches third grade, but I won't say what they call her. About ten minutes later, Principal opens the door, walks into his office, and welcomes Big Junior.

"Good to see you, Junior. Everybody's talking about that truck. You must be mighty proud of that shining jewel?"

Junior says, "Yeah, it's pretty highfalutin and drinks the dad-gum gas. I might have to get a second job just to buy fuel."

Principal says, "Junior, how can I help you?"

Big Junior does not have any refined social skills. In pool hall fights in his younger days, he is usually the victor. He does not intend on fighting the principal, but if he is going "to take somebody on" it didn't feel right to stay seated. He would fight if this did not go well. He felt too vulnerable in that chair, so he stands. Educated, highfalutin people discussed issues while seated. Real men stood, eye to eye, and settled their differences. Principal though didn't get out of his chair but encouraged Big Junior to sit down.

"How about a RC Cola? I got one in the refrigerator over there and got you a pack of peanuts if you want them?" Principal says. Big Junior because of the equipment breakdown and his workday cut short by the school visit has skipped lunch. He has not touched the can of sardines, saltine crackers, banana, and Moonpie in the brown bag in the truck.

Big Junior, thinking he might as well get something out of this office visit, says as he cracks his knuckles, "Sure. That's mighty nice of you Bull Dog." Everyone called Principal "Bull Dog" but not to his face. Bull Dog's face turns red as ketchup. He knew that's what people called him but only once before did a person call him Bull Dog to his face. It was Lenny Fox, and Bull Dog almost broke a big paddle over Lenny's buttocks hitting him so hard. Although he hikes his eyebrows, Principal controls himself and says, "Please call me James."

James hands Big Junior the cola and a pack of peanuts. "Thanks for the peanuts and *dope*." says Big Junior. In other parts of the country, soft drinks are called, soda, pop, or soda pop. I will never forget my amazement when I go down off the mountain in my teenage years and hear a person ask for a "bottle of pop." "What?" I wonder. In the mountains, a soft drink is a "dope." Some mountain amateur chemist, perhaps when Coca-Cola first came out, understood the drink was brewed with the leaves of the coca plant, which is also the source of cocaine, and started calling the drink a "dope."

Big Junior prepares a rare mountain delicacy. He gently pours, without spilling one nut, the pack of peanuts down into the small opening in the top of the "dope." He then sloshes down the first gulp of the RC Cola and peanuts-infused cocktail. For a moment, all is right in the world for Big Junior. Then he says, "James, I'm here because I hear Clyde has to sit on the other side of the room all by himself. It's hard enough to get him to come to school anyway. He wants to go up on the mountain and cut timber with me. I'll need him someday, but he needs to get some book-learning."

James says, "It's the ramps, Junior, it's the ramps. The other kids and the teacher just have a really hard time with . . .well, you know."

Big Junior says, "It ain't agin' the law to eat ramps." Then he takes another big swig of the RC Cola concoction and burps. "Sorry," he says "sometimes I forget I'm not in the woods." And he chuckles a little.

James says, "How about you take Clyde to work with you during ramp season? It's only a couple of weeks. Let him sit in the truck and read. And I will talk to his teacher and suggest to her that Clyde write a paper about logging or any part of the experience he wants. What do you think? And another thing I've been thinking about. You know, this school does not have much money. The poor teachers have to buy a lot of their own supplies. What if Clyde gathers ramps when he is up on the mountain with you? Then on Saturdays during ramp season, me and the teachers will have a ramp and scrambled egg breakfast here at the school for the community and charge 'em five dollars or something. Raise some money for the school."

Big Junior says, "James, I can go with that. Clyde would probably like it too."

James stands up, extends his hand. Big Junior does the same. They shake, and Big Junior says, "You're a pretty smart feller, that's what Clyde says too."

James thanks Big Junior for the compliment and starts toward the door. Then Big Junior says "You don't have another pack of 'em peanuts, do you?" A pack of peanuts and a "dope" save the day at Micaville Elementary School.

Alabama Bible Salesman
and Big Slim Blevins!

"As long as you live, keep learning how to live . . ."

SENECA

A FAMILY INVITES ME to Vacation Bible School as a ten-year-old, but even that was a theological and ethical disaster. The family inviting me has a son the same age as me. He is the VBS trouble maker and gets us into all kinds of trouble. We enter the first graders' room and break all their crayons, and into the kitchen when no one is looking and turn the cupcakes upside down, pushing until the icing squirted out the sides. Maybe Pastor Leroy was correct in his Howell prophesy.

Other than family funerals and weddings, I visit a church once as a teenager to see "the crying preacher." All the kids are doing it. A local Methodist preacher has Pseudobulbar Affect which causes him to cry spontaneously and uncontrollably. We are not interested in his sermon, but all the guys attend, two or three at a time, on Sunday mornings. The preacher with the super-sensitive amygdala in his brain starts crying at least once during the service, maybe when he talks about Jesus dying on the cross or about God's love. He always weeps through Holy Communion. We are simply voyeurs in our foolish youth. Some of the guys even place bets on when the crying preacher would lose control of his emotions during the service.

Bible salesmen from Alabama arrive in neighboring Burnsville the summer before my senior year in high school. Fortunately, they are not like one-eyed Big Dan, the Cyclops-like character in Coen Brothers' *Oh Brother Where Art Thou*, cleverly based on Homer's Greek epic *The*

Odyssey. Big Dan, played by John Goodman, takes a large branch and cold-cocks George Clooney and Tim Blake Nelson so that he might rob them. These Bible salesman are college students. This is a summer job. I don't think they got a coveted assignment in Burnsville. During the day they go from house to house "selling the Word of God."

Still not sixteen and without a driver's license, I am happy to show the godly but sometimes not so godly salesmen around in the evenings. We tour the pool halls and drive-in restaurants. I introduce them to young women in the area. One evening that summer, their car is full with the two Bible salesmen, myself, and three females, all high school drop-outs without sterling reputations. We were on our way to an overlook called Wiseman's View that looks out over the spectacular Linville Gorge. Bill (we jokingly called him "Bible Bill") is driving and not accustomed to mountain roads. A light rain falls on the road and mixes with motor oil that leaks from passing cars. Bible Bill hits one of the slick spots and slides off a bank into some trees below. No one is hurt. After making sure everyone is okay, I climb back to the road and stop the first car I see. The driver leaves to call the police. This is before cell phones, but the driver does not live too far away where he can use his land-line. There's a small cut on my head, and I'm a little dazed from it all. Another car comes by, and I instinctively stick out my thumb. The car stops. I explain the situation and ask if the driver will take me to the hospital. He agrees. I am not injured enough to go to the emergency room, just sorely embarrassed to be in a late-night car crash on a remote road with two Bible-salesman from Alabama and three locally notorious females.

Discharged from the emergency room, a hospital employee takes me home. The next morning I learn the lesson of not "leaving the scene of an accident." The local sheriff comes to our house and tells my parents about my unlawful behavior the night before. I insist that I had to get to the emergency room. The sheriff skeptical of my story warns me about the law I have broken, climbs into his cruiser, and leaves. Another lesson learned in the folly of youth.

Since this is open-faced mining country, drills strike underground spring water, and the mine fills up with water. Landowners often stock the mine holes with fish, and they grow large in the fresh cool water. Duck Hensley has a large mine hole on his property. One of the guys in our group, Leonard, boasts that Duck is his uncle, and he has his uncle's permission to fish in the mine hole. Duck's mine hole is legendary for its large fish, but Duck doesn't let many people fish there. Dennis and I know

Leonard is not telling the truth, but we want to fish in that mine hole so much we go along with the falsehood.

We hike the mile or so through the woods to the mine hole since we do not want anyone to see us entering the well-marked private property. Pristine blue water looks a mile deep. We haven't been fishing more than fifteen minutes when a white pick-up truck pulls up to the front side of the mine hole. We are fishing on the opposite side. Leonard screams, "It's Duck Hensley! Run!" We are not surprised by the command to flee because we know he doesn't have permission for us to be there. So we run. I don't even reel in my line. I run toward the woods behind us. As I run, the fishing line comes out of the water. Soon, it catches on a limb of a bush and snaps. I look over my shoulder, Mr. Hensley is closing in on Leonard and Dennis. I push deeper into the woods. Soon, I put a lot of distance between me and the pond as I tear through the woods. As I make my way over that small mountain, I see the cuts and scratches and feel the pain from the briars and thorns I have run through in my escape. I am not apprehended and grateful for that. I think if I make my way over the high ridge above me and then go down to the Toe River and walk down the river that Mr. Hensley cannot track me through water. A cunning and brilliant plan until I emerge from the river that runs by my house, climb the bank, and see Duck Hensley sitting on the front porch with my father. Mr. Hensley caught Leonard and Dennis. They give up my name. Luckily, my father and Duck are old acquaintances. Duck asks my father to give me a "good talkin to." After Duck leaves, my father starts laughing and asks me if it was worth all the cuts, scratches, and bruises. I admit that another lesson has been learned. Forgiven.

All the guys smoke cigarettes. Certainly, I should as well. I want to fit in. My peers have their drivers' licenses and drive to buy their Lucky Strikes, Pall Malls, and Marlboros. I have to stay at home and plot a way to smoke. A neighborhood pal brings me a pack of Cool Menthols. After he departs, I realize he didn't bring matches. Watching until my mother is in the rear of the house and away from the kitchen, I sneak into the kitchen and turn on a burner. Bending over to light the cigarette on the hot burner, my mother walks into the room. Deeply disappointed in me, she quietly and calmly talks to me about the perils and risks of smoking. Ashamed, I listen and never smoke again. Forgiven and redeemed at least from smoking by a loving mother.

When old enough to hitchhike, my friends and I thumb a ride to Spruce Pine and spend an afternoon in one of the pool halls. Built into the side of the mountain, Spruce Pine has an upper street and a lower street, and a pool hall on each street. The upper street pool hall is larger, has more tables, but that also meant more "young bucks" (as young men in the area were often called at the time) with testosterone-fed energy. Arguments erupt with screaming accusations like, "You cheated!" (meaning the other player had moved the cue ball from its proper place on the table to gain an advantage). Fistfights break out because sometimes paychecks are bet on the billiard game results.

When a fight did break out, it is usually quickly decided. Some of the guys are skilled fighters. Most grew up fist-fighting with brothers, cousins, and sometimes fathers. Chet Burleson's father physically abused him for years with slaps and even fists to the face. Chet's mother was a tall, large-boned woman, and he fortunately had his mother's DNA. By the time he was fourteen, Chet was bigger than his father and "the worm turned" as Chet began to get the upper hand in the frequent fist-fights. The Department of Social Services intervened at the mother's request and had the father removed from the home before Chet did his father some real damage.

I still remember the sound of a powerful fist striking a jaw in pool hall fights. When the fist strikes the jaw, a loud "pop" shoots across the room. The head snaps violently to the side. In lots of cases, it's game-set-match because the other guy knows he is outmatched.

Alton "Nose" Jones "racks" in the lower street pool room. A rack is the employee of the pool hall. At the end of the game, he racks the balls for the next game. He uses a hollow triangle to arrange the balls into the triangle fixture of balls on the table for the next "break" (a break is when the first player strikes the rack of balls on the table with the cue ball). No more glorious moment exists than to yell across the noisy pool hall, "Rack 'em Nose!" because that means you won the game. Only the winner of the game gets to proclaim "Rack 'em!"

The lower street pool hall normally proves more civil than the upper street pool hall where fights often break out. The reason is the owner, Skip Ballew (also the owner of a local tire store), stops by at least a couple of times a day and warned the patrons, "If you boys fight in my pool hall, I will law you!" We knew what he meant. He would call the police.

Alton Jones in his younger days plays pool in the upper street pool hall. He is accused of cheating in a game. Heated denials and accusations are exchanged. Al's opponent Rufus Conley is big and muscular, working three days a week at a sawmill stacking lumber all day and playing pool the rest of the week. Rufus's boss lets him work three days because he does the work of five days in three. He got hot one summer in the pool hall and took his shirt off. Guys said he had enough hair on his massive chest to make a Persian rug. Rufus's huge fists are as hard as bowling balls. Rufus lands a mighty right fist violently on Al's nose, thrusting his nose permanently to the right side of Al's face. The soft cartilage and tissue in Al's nose easily bent to one side. For the rest of his days, Al's nose is dramatically flattened to the right side of his face. Like many of the mountain people, Al does not have insurance or the money to see a doctor. Thus, the imprint of four knuckles is forever imprinted on Al's twisted nose.

One winter afternoon with school canceled because of deep snow, Dennis and I hitchhike a ride to the upper street pool room. (We once missed an entire month of school because the snow was so deep. When it melted during the day, it would freeze back on the roads by morning. The highway department would not allow the buses on the icy mountain back roads.) We play on one of the tables near the front door when the door slams open, almost coming off its hinges. In steps an angry young man, Cotton Cresson, in his early twenties who declares, "If anyone tries to leave, I'll kill you!" Cotton is looking for Ned Briggs. "Is Ned Briggs in here? The son-of-a-bitch stole my wife, my young'un, and my truck. I am going to put him in the ground!" Apparently, Cotton lost big-time in a divorce suit. Fortunately, Ned is not in the pool hall this afternoon. The raging young man storms out the door, swearing to find Ned, and kill him.

In the upper street pool hall, the racking job belongs to Big Slim Blevins. At least six feet-five inches tall, Big Slim weighs maybe "a buck-fifty-five." He has kyphosis, an exaggerated forward rounding of the back (also called hunchback). Ichabod Crane-like, locals say Big Slim is like a scarecrow escaped from a field. Everyone loves Big Slim and rewards him with generous tips. When he goes out of town though, he always seems to get in trouble.

Residents of neither Burnsville nor Spruce Pine enjoy fast food restaurants at the time. The owner of the pool hall sends Big Slim and another employee to Charlotte to pick up a new pool table. They have never been to any fast-food places and stop at a McDonald's outside Charlotte. A tussle between Big Slim and the manager occurs when Big Slim orders fried chicken and the clerk says they don't have fried chicken. Big Slim makes a scene when he starts yelling that he has never been in a restaurant before that didn't have fried chicken.

The manager explains his restaurant is part of a nation-wide chain and has to follow the national menu. Big Slim gives the manager "a good cussin." The owner says he is "offended." Slim Blevins "balls up his fist" and says, "I will offend you with this!" The other pool hall employee tries to be the peacemaker, "Slim, let's go on up the road and find us some fried chicken." Big Slim, seething with anger, snorts out, "If I had my druthers, I'd knock his teeth out. He don't need 'em if he ain't got no chicken!" Slim turns and storms out of the restaurant but not before kicking over a life-size poster-stand of Ronald McDonald. For years, Slim Blevins is teased in the pool hall as the only person in the world to get into a fight with Ronald McDonald.

Big Slim considers "maters" (tomatoes) and mater-sandwiches true delicacies. He once got into a fight with a cousin over which sandwich spread was best on a mater-sandwich. Big Slim loved Duke's mayonnaise while the cousin always used Hellman's. Big Slim got the cousin down on the ground and held him in a half-nelson choke-hold for over thirty minutes until the cousin agreed Duke's was the best.

Big Slim enters and wins a drawing sponsored by a regional car dealership chain. His prize is a pair of tickets to the 1960 NBA All-Star Game played in Philadelphia with NBA greats Bill Russell and Wilt Chamberlain. His tickets also included passes to join Wilt Chamberlain at his pre-game meal. Big Slim created a stir when he told game officials "I don't eat with colored people."

In those days, African-Americans stayed to themselves in small communities around Burnsville and Spruce Pine. They had their own schools, and a white person could go about a life-time without encountering a person of color. Asheville about an hour away was a different story and also the scene of lunch counter scenes and protests. When we turn sixteen, Dennis and I take our first big road trip and attend a Ray Charles concert in the Asheville Civic Center. We were one of the few white people to attend. When we got home late that evening, we learned that Martin Luther King Jr. had been murdered at 6:05 PM at the Lorraine Hotel in Memphis, but no one at the concert seemed to know because this was before cell phones. We suspected the mood in the Civic Center might have been alarming different had the audience known.

Before we had our drivers' licenses and during the boring summers, we catch the 8:30 AM bus that came through Newdale and arrived in Asheville later in the morning. Conveniently, the return bus has us home by 6:00 PM, making for a fun day for a couple of culturally deprived teenagers. The most popular men's clothing store in Asheville is The Men's Store. We do not often have the money to make a purchase, but we love gawking at the fine shirts, slacks, and coats on the racks. One afternoon in the store admiring and daydreaming about the fine attire on display, we are told that we have to leave the store in fifteen minutes. We asked why we had to leave? The salesman, aloofly, informs us that Reverend Billy Graham (who lived in the nearby town of Black Mountain) is coming to the store and requested complete privacy for his shopping. Leaving the store and walking down the street, we joked to each other, "I don't guess Billy Graham wants to preach to us today." "Yeah, we don't have to sing 'Just As I Am.'"

Interest in playing sports, athletics saves me from a life-long career in the pool halls, a fate that falls upon many of the young men. It is a great outlet to join the other students on the ball-field during recess or after school. A little league team is fun with the other boys from Micaville Elementary School until we begin night games. I play the outfield and catching fly-balls is never a problem during the day, but at night I can't find the ball in the giant lights around the field. Fly balls drop all around me because I pick up their descent too late. Parents and fans of opposing teams laugh in delight as I let their kids get on base and cross home plate. Parents of my team scream at me "just catch the damn ball!" I need glasses but have never been examined.

For a running back in football, great vision, though helpful, is not a requirement. I take a helmet to school, and during recess I am coached by an eighth-grade teacher. He takes an interest in me and assures me that I will be a high school football star when the time comes. The next year I will be a freshman at East Yancey High School. The school system has now modernized. New high schools have been built, and Micaville School is now an elementary school through the eighth grade.

High school football practice starts two weeks before school starts. I can't wait. I buy my own cleats, but the school furnishes the uniforms. The owner of the shoe store warns me "Aren't you too young to play high school football?" I am only twelve years old, having started first grade at four. I don't think about that, until the first day after practice in the showers. I have an embarrassing problem. I have not gone through puberty, and everyone else has. No pubic hair, ouch. The other guys in the ninth grade are fourteen or older and don't have that problem. It is a small high school with only one team, not a varsity and a junior varsity. I am twelve, practicing with guys eighteen and some older. I compete to some extent on the field but not in the showers. So I stop taking a shower after practice. I always grab a locker in the corner, so I can change quickly without exposing myself to other guys.

My football comes to a merciful ending. I play tailback on the practice squad. The quarterback calls a toss sweep. After the center snaps the ball to him, he pitches the ball to me as I run to the outside. I put a beautiful fake on the defensive end and get around him. The cornerback comes up to stop me. I start to put a move on him. The defensive end recovers and comes up behind me. The strong defensive end, embarrassed by my fake, pulls me backward violently. My legs are caught underneath me. My right knee explodes. Teammates drag me off the field. We don't have a trainer, let alone a doctor. I crawl to the locker room, get dressed, and say goodbye to my football career.

I recover enough to try out for the basketball team in November. Practice goes well. I think I have earned a spot on the team. The coach is a busy man, teacher, athletic director, football coach, and basketball coach. He has to select his squad from among the tryouts. He tells us to sit on the bleachers. He retrieves a large duffle bag and stands in front of us. I do not know what is to happen, no one does. He starts throwing uniforms at certain players but apparently not caring ultimately who gets a uniform. Coach looks at me. He wants me to have a uniform, I think at that moment. A uniform is up in the air and headed my way. I wait for it to arrive. Larry Jones sits beside me. He is not a good basketball player, slow and plodding. This time, he is quick to rise and grabs the uniform. Coach throws a few more uniforms in the air, none in my direction. When he has finished the random throwing, he says "You guys with uniforms. We practice after sixth period tomorrow." He walks away to his busy life.

Devastated, I sit on my rear and let Larry get "my" uniform. The uniform is destined for me, but my passivity, sitting down and waiting for it come to me, leaves me empty handed and wondering what might have been. Painful, it is a valuable lesson for life. I am now determined never to sit passively as life passes me by.

The basketball team that year wins the district championship and advances to the state tournament in Raleigh. It is a first for any mountain high school team, basketball or football. The team might have won the state championship. These mountain boys are talented. An older brother of one of the players shows up at the team hotel in Raleigh with bottles of liquor. The players drink heavily the night before the game. They are also fascinated with fire extinguishers and elevators they have never seen before. They spend most of the night chasing and spraying each other with fire extinguishers. When they tire of that, they ride elevators and invent an elevator race game, using two different elevators. Not surprisingly, they lose their game the next day but return to Burnsville that evening with great elevator stories.

The Wild Side of Angels

"I'm a goddam minor."

J.D. SALINGER, *THE CATCHER IN THE RYE*

SHORTLY AFTER NOT MAKING the high school basketball team, I experience a shaking event that I did not see coming. The French teacher rents a bus. French class students in our high school are invited to make a field trip to a French restaurant in Pinehurst, NC. Hours from Burnsville in the mountains to Pinehurst in the southern piedmont, we leave early in the morning. At this point in my life, I have not been more than forty miles from home. Our family takes maybe a once-a-year trip to Asheville but only if someone else drives. My parents aren't comfortable driving in the city.

We arrive at the French restaurant that field trip day. The teacher makes us order in French. The food is fine, but I don't understand what the big deal is. I could be just as happy having a cheeseburger at the drive-in restaurant, Little Smoky, in Burnsville. The trip home in the dark bus though is eventful. As a now barely thirteen-year-old freshman, I sit near the front of the bus. A young woman taps on my shoulder, a senior, attractive with straight glossy blonde hair falling on her shoulders and deep, rich blue eyes. She is part of the "in" group from the town of Burnsville. A curvaceous figure and a sweet demeanor, I've noticed her in the halls at high school but never dared approach her. I live in a rural area of Yancey County. We are poor, and my parents work in the mine and in the local sweat factory. This young woman and her friends in the back of the bus are from the upper class of Burnsville. Parents are doctors, dentists, merchants, bankers. I don't have a clue why they want me in the back of the bus. She speaks gently and smiles warmly as she encourages me to the back of the bus.

Dark in the rear of the bus, I see at least a half dozen, attractive, junior and senior young women on the long back seat of the bus that stretches from one side of the bus to the other, with just enough room for me in the middle. The young woman who brought me to the back of the bus tells me that they want to teach me how to kiss! I don't know what to say. Before I can say anything, she plants her lips on mine. Stunned at first, I find her lips warm and moist. I like it, although I am much more than surprised at what is happening. Seconds later her tongue is searching for my tongue. Like me, my tongue is shy. I resist, but her tongue keeps exploring. She pulls away and says "Not bad, you just need to use your tongue a little more."

Jean jumps in next. She puts her arms around me too, and her entire body touches my body as her lips meet mine. She is warm, soft, and keeps pulling me closer and closer. Her skin velvety, Sarah joins their fun. I start to breathe heavily. Sarah giggles as she momentarily pulls away and says, "You're getting aroused, aren't you?" All the young women laugh. They continue to pass me around. Betsy kisses me, and then goes for my neck, gets some of my skin between her front teeth, and grinds my skin. The next morning I discover my first "hickies." On the bus, feelings collide in me. I enjoy this but quiver inside. I did not expect this terror and pleasure at the same time. Betsy asks, "Do you like it?" In a shrill voice, I say, "Yes." When they all have their way with me, I make my way up the aisle to my seat near the front. I hear gales of giggles coming from the other students on the bus. I shake like jello inside but sense something at the molecular level is happening with me. Yep, hormones unleashed! I hear the kissers laughing behind me. Gang kissed, my innocence is over. Part of me wanted to be home, playing with model cars or something, and part of me enjoyed the warm lips and soft bodies. I experienced the "wild side of angels."

I reside in a different social class than these young women and the cool guys of the "Burnsville Bourgeoise" as my family is not as well off as the Burnsville "in" group. This reality becomes acutely aware to me one day at school. President Lyndon B. Johnson embarks on the Great Society Program. Part of this program is assistance to Appalachian poverty families. A free dental program for students from below-poverty level families is established and made available through the schools. I am in Gilbert Cox's history class. Each classroom has a speaker on the wall near the ceiling for the school's intercom system. Over the speaker, the principal says, "We're going to read a list of students whose families' incomes are below the poverty level. You are to report to the gym for a free dental exam." He starts reading the names in alphabetical order. My dread increases. The cool kids' names are not read. The principal is in the F's, then the G's. I hope and pray he does not read my name. I slide down into my desk as my name is announced. My face flushes hot red. I decide not to go. Mr. Cox sees I am not going to the gym. "David Howell, you going to the gym?" I shake my head, "No." He resumes his lecture. I feel branded. All the cool kids know now because of this Gestapo-like proclamation that I am poor. It is intense shame. Anger burns in me that they read our names. Don't they know how embarrassing that is?

The author Toni Morrison, in an interview, talked about growing up in the Jim Crow-Old South. She always had "a little white man on her shoulder" watching her all the time to make sure she did not get "too uppity." I know a something about that feeling. For me, it was "a little rich kid on my shoulder" who always has a lot more money, better clothes, lives in a fancy house, and drives a new car. My parents felt a kind of socio-economic "racism." They would never dine at some of the resort restaurants in the area. Their dining was not forbidden, but they were concerned they would be looked down on and feel uncomfortably "out of place."[4]

Sometimes, I feel like I am in the "in" group. I get invited to some things, others times not. The girls say "I am cute." I don't know how to take that at first. Babies are cute. Puppies are cute. I eventually realize it is one thing in my favor.

As a sophomore, a young woman in the senior class invites me to the "Junior-Senior prom." Although not sure I should be doing this, I accept. Since I don't have a drivers' license, I arrange to double date with one of her friends. Anxiety festers in me as I think about the banquet before the dance. I hear there are several forks to choose from and how do I know which one to use first? What if there are several spoons? And dancing? Am I a good enough dancer for the junior-senior group? Yikes!

In our sophomore year, all my friends turn sixteen and have their drivers' licenses. I will not be sixteen until I am a senior, a painful waiting. Sometimes, guys offer to give me a ride to an event or a game. Other times I ride with my parents, embarrassed.

Eager to be driven, my car sits in the driveway. I am just not old enough to drive. I save for a car starting as a ten-year-old. A car is a magic carpet to escape the mountains. I work at Uncle's grocery on Saturdays and save some money. Summer vacations are always boring. Parents are always busy and exhausted, working the mine and factory and "raising a garden." We never take a family vacation because of my parents' fatigue and because we have no money. Parents work their entire lives at minimum wage and send three kids to college, a remarkable feat, but no money for trips. I watch as neighbors drive away to beach vacations and other faraway places. I can only imagine.

In the spring before my thirteenth birthday, my father announces an opportunity for me. The mine has long abandoned a quarter-mile stretch of buried pipe, and he has permission to dig it up for resale. So all summer long I go to the mine. My mother packs my lunch, identical to my father's: apple, fig bar, and a Spam (cheap canned meat) sandwich. Spam and Treet kept a lot of mountain families alive back in the day. Interestingly, poor Asian-American families in cities across America ate Spam as well, chopping it up for a stir-fry. I read an article recently about a successful chef and restaurant owner in San Francisco who still has Spam once a week as a "hard-time meal of remembrance."

At 6:00 AM, my father and I walk to the road. Minutes later Red Moore in his green panel van stops in front of us. Red gutted the inside of the van and installed three rows of crude benches, not comfortable but serve the purpose of getting the needed muscle to the mines. For a small fee, he picks up several workers along the way. We are the next to last stop. Pappy Price and several others are already on board. Sweet Tater is the last worker to be picked up. It is not hard to figure out why James Honeycutt is called Sweet Tater. His baby-like face is decorated with glowing red cheeks, a perpetual smile from ear to ear, and a small whiff of blonde hair sits on top of his head. Probably fifty pounds overweight, he always wears denim overalls with suspenders crossing over his shoulders. His voice is high-pitched like a little boy's.

Red Moore transports over half the mine's workers. Not an eighth-grade education among this band of miners, it is a brotherhood, a fraternity, of uneducated men with a life of back-breaking hard work in front of them. Conscientiousness flowing through his veins, Red leaves home extra early and arrives at the mine one hour before work time, saying if he has a flat tire on the way he can still get the crew to the mine on time.

Red stops and lets me off just before he gets to the mine and processing plant. My excavation project is on top of a small mountain where it is as quiet as a lonely, country cemetery. I hike through the woods with lunch-bucket in hand. My father and I pre-positioned my tools: ax, hoe, pickaxe and two kinds of shovels (square and pointed). The pipe is in the ground for twenty years. Several feet deep, roots grow over and around much of it. Digging through rocks as well, I labor away, slowing unearthing section after section. At 3:00 PM, I trek down the mountain to board Red's old green panel wagon. This is my routine Monday through Friday. At the end of the summer, the pipes are sold. We open up my first bank account.

With other part-time jobs during the school year, soon, I have enough money to buy a car, at least this one. My father's boss at the mine has a 1956 Chevrolet for sale since he is buying a new car. He wants three hundred dollars. I have three hundred and eighteen dollars. So at fourteen, I have my first car, but I can't drive it. It sits in the driveway for nearly two years. I give it an occasional washing. At fifteen years and six months, a learner's permit means I can drive with a licensed driver. Liberating light is at the end of the tunnel! One of the most exhilarating days of my life comes on my sixteenth birthday. My mother takes me to the DMV office. I take the driving tests. Successful, I drive to school! Two years of agonizing waiting are over. It's freedom!

In few days, I visit the barbershop in Spruce Pine. A distance relative by marriage has cut my hair for several years.

"Your mother is not with you?" Jonas asks since until now my mother drives me to a haircut.

"Nope, I got my license last Monday." I say.

"Wait a minute," he says, "this calls for a celebration." He goes into a back room and emerges with a big grin on his face and a quart-size mason jar. Unscrewing the top, he takes a big swallow and blows the air out of his mouth as he hands it to me.

"What's that?" I quiz him.

"That's shine. Take a big swaller. You're a man now!"

Manhood stings the inside of my mouth for several minutes for I downed moonshine for the first and last time.

Friends drive new cars. The old Chevy is fine by me. It is black and white, two doors, and would be a valuable antique if still in existence, but certainly swallowed and crushed by a car compacter many years ago. It is an automatic, equipped with a six-cylinder engine. A heavy car, tank-like, with a steering wheel that is huge by today's fashionable standards. Overdrive engages if the gas pedal is held all the way to the floor. My friends laugh at my overdrive. I sink the gas pedal to the floor. The engine roars, but surprisingly the car does not pick up speed. It is comical.

A cool white morning of frost and fog, we ride to school. My friends will not laugh this time when I go into overdrive. Mike, Gary, and Dennis ride with me. I get teased a lot for driving too slowly. On the way to school this foggy morning of dim vision, we are behind a school bus, that without a car we would be riding. The guys are impatient following that bus. East Yancey High School sits on top of a ridge. At the bottom of the two-lane highway leading up to the school is a railroad crossing. The school bus has to stop at the crossing. The black and white '56 Chevy is the first car behind the bus with a long string of cars behind us that nearly white-out morning.

The guys swear later they didn't encourage me to pass. When the bus pulls away from the crossing, I pull out to pass. I slam the gas pedal to the floor. The car roars like a steel-bellied beast, but incredibly slows down because we are starting up the hill. Out of the fog ahead of us appears a massive dump truck, loaded with tons of heavy gravel, and headed directly toward us with nowhere to go but into and through us. In that instant, it does not look good for us. I don't have time to look, but I imagine the students in the bus alongside us see the crushing and bloody calamity about to happen before their eyes. I don't have time to think. I glance to the left. In the fog is a driveway up to a house on the left-hand side of the road. Instinctively, I whip the big steering wheel to the left and up the driveway. The car stops on the driveway incline, and the dump truck loudly but harmlessly passes below us. We look at the bus. A celebration breaks out. At the windows, students cheer and clap. We sit in the car for a few minutes. Luckily alive, we go on to another day at school. I dodge in the nick of time Reverend Leroy's curse of eternity in Hell.

A year later during my freshman year at college, I head back to campus after a weekend visit home. Harry, from one of the few African-American families in that part of the mountains and who attends the same college, asks for a ride back to campus. It is a cold, rainy night as we travel the two-lane highway that leads through Burnsville, Asheville, Waynesville, to campus. The trip is two hours in total. We are in the first segment of the trip near the little community of Swiss when we cross over the mountain that causes US Route 19-E to rise up and then wind down toward Asheville.

Rain slicks the asphalt, and visibility is poor. Coming around a curve, a flashing blue light reflects off the watery road in front of us. A state trooper is pulled off the road up ahead. An accident looms in front of us. A car slid off the road, down a bank, and hangs precariously above the gorge below. I panic and slam on the brakes. Our family is poor. Car tires are not changed unless the car will not pass state safety inspection. Only then do we get new tires, usually recapped tires. When I hit the brakes, the bald tires do not grip the wet road. The car goes into an immediate slide. I sit frozen at the wheel. I do not know what to do. Soon the car spins completely around and slides backward. We slide past the state trooper, holding a flashlight, standing where the car is off the bank. He flashes the light in my face as I go by him backward! The car continues its slow spin and miraculously rights itself in the proper lane going in the correct direction. Just as miraculously no car comes from the other direction, or else a disastrous outcome.

Later, I wonder what the trooper thought as a white guy and a black guy in a black and white Chevy go by him backwards down that steep mountain road on the dark rainy night. He did not jump in his cruiser and come after us. Maybe he had a more serious incident on his hands with the car on the crevice of the gorge. Or maybe he could not believe what his eyes just saw: a car coming backwards down a steep mountain road, incredibly righting itself, and speeding away. Maybe he thought I am destined to be a NASCAR driver? The truth is I did nothing, frozen in my seat.

Later the same year I arrive home for Christmas break. My mother schedules a dental appointment for me the first day home because I start work at the mine the next day to earn "spending money" for the remainder of the academic year. We never heard of fluoride, and cavities were a constant problem. Summer work at the mine was not too bad, but it was deathly cold at the mine in December. Working outside, it didn't take long for the temperatures in the teens or single digits to make the hands and feet hurt like a bastard. So I am glad to have one more day inside a warm house or car.

Early that morning, I speed along toward the town of Spruce Pine and the dentist. This part of the highway is a straight-a-way. A large bank is up to the right, making that part of the road on the north side. The winter sun, staying low in the sky, rarely shines on the road. Moisture from the day before freezes overnight. In the early hours of the morning, the sun does not shine there to melt the slick mass. Many cars with good tires pass through that morning with no problems. When my slick tires come into contact with the part of the road where the sun never shines, I once again go into a slide. Like before, I am immediately in a three-sixty degree spin. Traveling backward, and following the same script, the car comes all the way around. I keep going. Incredibly once again, there are no cars coming toward me in the other lane. A few minutes later, a little pain from the needle and drill in the dentist's chair is nothing compared to what might have happened. I capture lightning in a bottle again, barely escaping death and Reverend Leroy's curse.

The above near-death experiences, some of which certainly shaped me theologically, are not the first or the last for me. Before my hard-working parents could afford a tricycle, I have a horse. The horse is only as fast as I am and never needs feeding or watering. The horse is the long wooden stem of a kitchen mop that I inherit once the mop loses most of its' thick and, by then, smelly threads. I put the stick-horse between my legs, confidently shout "Giddy-Up," and away we go. A cowboy hat, boots, and a silver six-shooter in a black holster on my waist make me the toughest, fastest cowboy-child in Boonford. If 'ole Daniel Boone comes through Boonford now, he will certainly show due respect to this good-guy lawman.

Many adventures occur in the woods and up the steep mountain behind our house. There could be an Indian behind any tree. Bears and mountain lions best flee when the stick-horse named "Silver" and his dashing, bold rider come up the trail. One afternoon, Silver and I are coming down the trail "like a scalded dog." (This is an old mountain saying that originated unfortunately when people cooked outside and a dog nosing around to get scraps from under a table might accidentally turn over a pot of boiling water. The pain sends the yelping dog into a flight syndrome.) We are going fast when horse and rider jump the little stream that flows from our spring house and down the mountainside. Up a little bank and through the front yard, we speed as if we have wings of angels. Into the backyard, we see family members gathered around my father's '59 white Chevrolet Impala. Someone left the front passenger door open. As the speeding Silver nears the protruding car door, the accomplished rider makes one serious mistake. My right foot gets entangled with the stick-horse. Momentum propels the rider forward, head first, like a diver sprung from a diving board. Head meets the side of car door, unfortunately not the smooth outside of the door, but the inside, sharp edge of the door meant to be firmly and safely shut against the body of the car. As with most head wounds, blood flushes on the door, on the ground, down my face, chest, and legs. I am alive, breathing, but out cold.

My father drives toward the hospital in Burnsville. My mother sits in the back seat with me. I "come around" in a few miles.

"Where are we going?" I scream.

"The hospital." My mother says.

"Are they going to put in stitches?" I ask.

My mother makes a crucial mistake and says, "Yeah, probably."

I let out a blood-curdling scream. "No!!! No stitches! It will hurt!"

I thrash about, still bleeding from the head. My mother argues with me about how important it is to get stitches and how I will have a terrible, ugly scar the rest of my life without stitches.

"I don't care about a scar!" I declare, among more blood-throwing thrashing.

"All right, all right. Calm down." My father says. He turns the car around and heads back home. Once again, I throw a fit and get my way. I am a powerful little boy with head bandages for weeks, and yes, a scar for life, although wrinkles and aging spots hide most of it now, nature's cosmetology.

Scary, traumatic events happen all around me. Late one afternoon, the phone rings. It is my father's sister who lives at the head of Roaring Creek. Her husband is "known to take a drink" but is trying to "get sober." Unfortunately, the uncle is "back on the sauce." Liquored up and impulsive, he goes gallivanting to Spruce Pine and decides to call on an old girlfriend. Her husband happens to have the day off from work and is home when this uncle comes calling. It begins with a verbal argument. Then the two take feeble swings at each other. Neither land a punch. The jealous husband picks up a three-foot piece of two by four and lands a blow to uncle's forehead. My aunt tells us that an ambulance takes her husband to the emergency room. He is alive, but his skull is open. For weeks, nightmares of open skulls wake me in the middle of the night.

I remember this only vaguely, but my parents told me I had an imaginary trucking business as a young tycoon. With small plastic shovels, I load up toy trucks with dirt that is mined from a bank along our road and send my imaginary drivers, Tackhead, Saucerhead, and Churnhead off to deliver.

Every fall before "cold weather," a real dump truck delivers a load of coal. We heat our house with coal burned in a pot-bellied stove. The stove glows red from the intense heat. Later we get a Warm Morning, a Cadillac of stoves that looks like a piece of furniture since the firebox is surrounded by a lovely dark brown metal case. As a child, my job is to bring in the coal in an old, rusty, black cold bucket. I begrudgingly fulfill my duty every afternoon after school and before the supper of pinto beans, usually with a side of cornbread. Often, we crumble the cornbread into a glass of milk ("sweet" or "sour") and stir it around with a spoon until a thick blend is achieved. "Cornbread and milk smoothies" nourished many hungry mountain farmers and miners.

As a little boss man with my own trucking crew, I wait eagerly on the top of the bank above the road that runs in front of our house on coal delivery day. Black smoke boils out of the Mack Truck's smokestack as the driver gears down the diesel engine as he approaches our driveway. Up the driveway he comes, and my eyes are big as dinner plates.

The same driver comes every year, Royce "Yellow Jacket" Conley. He was dubbed Yellow Jacket because he stopped his dump truck on the side of the road one summer day and went off into the bushes to do his business. Regrettably, he does not see the nickel-sized hole in the ground. After dropping his trousers and underwear, he squats over the hole. The hole is the front door for an abnormally large bees' nest. With the first sting on his buttocks, Royce panics. Bees are now buzzing all around him. Stinging around his rectum, his backside is soon covered with pain-inflicting yellow-jackets. Trying to get up, his feet catch in his trousers. He falls backward. His naked legs, buttocks, face, and arms (it is summer and he is wearing a short-sleeve shirt) are now being used for sting practice by hundreds of bees. He finally rights himself, shuffles away. While beating off the bees, he pulls up his pants. Back at the road, he hails a passing car driven by ole man Terrell Silver. Terrell, still a good driver, rushes Royce to Burnsville hospital in record time, saving his life.

Royce "Yellow Jacket" Conley, to the delight of a little boy and his imaginary crew of drivers, backs the bellowing diesel dump truck to the same spot he dumps the coal every year. Plumes of black smoke from the truck's stack rise into the air as the bed of the truck rises. Large coal chunks hit the ground. Coal is "from off somewhere." Coal is not a prevalent mineral in western North Carolina. The geology gods only put coal farther north and west in the mountains of Virginia and especially in West Virginia and Kentucky. Railroad coal-cars bring the black ore into the depot near Spruce Pine, and local coal merchants sell and make deliveries to homes in the area.

Late afternoon, after the morning delivery and after my crew and I spent the day moving coal from one side of the coal pile to the other, I walk through the back door that goes directly into the kitchen of our house. I sit down before my bowl of pinto beans, cornbread, and milk. My father says, "Looks like you have been having fun in that coal pile." I proudly say, "Yep, got a lot of work done. Even got some blasting done. I found a blasting cap in the pile and used it several times. I guess you heard the explosions." Everyone at the table chuckles. After supper, my father walks out to the barn to "slop the hogs." Slop is leftover food and grain mixed with water in five-gallon buckets. Twenty minutes later my father walks back into our house and with raised eyebrows says, "You know that dynamite blasting cap we thought Dave was pretending to have found? Well, it really is one. Lucky that boy didn't get blown to pieces. It must have been scooped up at the coal mine with a big load of coal." Lightning caught in a bottle again.

"Lucky" To Be Alive!

"Life is a balance of holding on and letting go."

RUMI

I LOVED MY ADVENTURES on the stick-horse, Silver. When I am eleven, I get a real horse, a dangerous bargain basement horse it turns out. Horseback riding becomes all the rage in the area for those who could afford fine riding horses. Uncle Lee buys three Arabians. Uncle Ray purchases a herd of Arabians. Lee and Ray open retail stores in Spruce Pine after World War II. Ray has a hardware business, later sells, and opens a real estate office. Lee has a furniture store. They are both incredibly successful businessmen and much beloved by the community. Everyone is talking about the trail rides taken by Ray and Lee and their families. I am too old for a stick-horse at this time, so I can only wonder what it would be like to ride a horse, let alone own one.

My father, an emotionally distant and occasionally abusive man, experienced his own difficult childhood, and so his parenting and nurturing skills were limited, as was his money. Laborers like him and my mother work paycheck to paycheck and are paid minimum wage their entire lives. Every other Friday is payday at the mine. As soon as my father gets out of Red Moore's worker carrying truck-van on those Friday afternoons, Jack Howell makes the short walk to Uncle's store and hands him the check. Uncle pulls out the dun-book, subtracts the amount due for charges during the last two weeks from the check, and hands Jack his dangerously hard-earned small amount of money.

Money's tight. Sometimes we wear small, misfitting, old shoes until we can afford new ones. But my father does the unexpected. He must have loved me is the only explanation. He goes to his brother Ray, and borrows $150.00 to buy me a horse! The problem is, even in that day, you could not get much of a horse for $150.00. It would have to be a "senior citizen" horse, or it could be Lucky! Lucky is fully grown, about five years old. As I find out later, Lucky is not so lucky.

Lucky arrives, a big strong, golden palomino, probably a Tennessee Walker or a combination of breeds. On a brilliant, sunny summer day, unbelievably, my dream comes true. Like my cousins, I have a horse. I proudly ride Lucky around the flat pasture outside Uncle Lee's barn. Uncle Lee has graciously allowed us to keep Lucky in his barn.

The weekend comes. Thrilled, I am invited on the Howell family trail ride with Uncles Ray, Lee, Woodrow, and the cousins. On Sunday afternoon the plan forms to ride down an old logging road along the South Toe River from Newdale to the backside of Presnell Holler that borders on the North Toe River. Then we follow a Native American trail to the gravel road out of Presnell Holler to Highway 80, not a highly traveled road, and back to Newdale. A wonderful leisure ride along the river as we leave civilization, we will not see a house for hours. The loggers blazed a narrow road into the wilderness along the river bank years ago. Now high weeds and small bushes reach toward the sky, but this is not a problem for the horses. It is peaceful and pleasant as most of the time we can hear the river flowing and sometimes roaring through rapids. Eventually, we reach the intersection of the logging road with the Native American trail that leads into Presnell Holler and the gravel road.

Presnell Holler, one of the hundreds of small communities in western North Carolina, was settled in the late 1700s and early 1800s by second-generation immigrants from Scotland, Ireland, Wales whose parents had first settled in Pennsylvania after fleeing persecution in England. Barefooted, blonde, and red-headed children, playing in the dirt outside their homes on this summer day, are their descendants.

The indigenous trail rises up over a mountain. Down the trail, we emerge into a gorgeous valley with fields of oats and corn bending in the gentle wind. In a fenced field, farm horses raise their heads, give us a curious glance before bending back down for another mouthful of green grass as they swish their tails from side to side. A spattering of high cirrus clouds decorates the brilliant blue sky. Bees buzz in the fields, songbirds twitter. A mule, head stuck out a barn door, brays at these invaders. Goats graze by a shabby old fence line. One of our horses whinnies as dogs bark. When they spot us, the children run out to greet us, this long line of horses and intergenerational riders.

The novice rider in the group, I bring up the rear. The group stops and dismounts. Uncle Ray spots a lovely blackberry patch. The berries are perfectly ripe and sweet as my mother's homemade chocolate candy. It is a spectacular day with perfect weather, bright sun but with the low humidity of the high mountains, and now a bounty of nature's delicious fruit. Buttocks sore but with some relief, we remount and continue the journey up the winding road to the top of the mountain, leaving the adorable children and now friendly dogs behind. Ahead are tall and straight poplar trees, standing like sentinels over the mountain pass ahead.

Unknown to me, the serendipitous blackberry patch stop is a bit of bad luck for me because the group does not plan to stop again until we reach Highway 80, probably an hour away on horseback. I proudly continue the rear support of the group. Fantasies run through my mind of being a trusted cavalry rider in the rear of General Lee's or General Grant's army.

We wind our way up the gravel road with horses swishing their tails and occasional steaming chunks of horse manure hitting the dusty gravel road. Uncle Ray reaches the summit. He continues on down the other side. All the riders and their mounts follow. Near the top, I notice my saddle is loose. I certainly do not want the saddle to slip to one side of the horse and put me in a precarious position. So at the summit, I stop to tighten my saddle.

Dismounted, I notice the last rider rounding a curve below and disappearing from my sight. This will not be a problem because I will catch up at the scheduled rest stop at the foot of the mountain. I notice the rear billet, or girth strap, that runs underneath Lucky's belly and attaches to each side of the saddle is indeed loose. I give the strap a firm tug and all is well. I take the reins in one hand, place my left foot in the left-side stirrup. I begin to swing my right leg over the saddle, and I plan to put my right foot in the right-side stirrup. But as my leg swings over the saddle, Lucky bolts. In seconds he's in full gallop! In those seconds, as my right leg is suspended over the saddle, I have a choice to make because Lucky's burst causes me to drop the reins! I can try to get off Lucky who is now streaking down the gravel road, or I can continue to mount. Without reins, I have little way of controlling him. I do have hold of the saddle horn so I swing my leg on over and get my foot into the other stirrup.

Lucky apparently developed an equine separation anxiety disorder. He did not seem restless at all when the other horses go ahead and as I was dismounted, tightening the girth strap. When I began to mount, it might have been a trigger for him that he could catch up with his family of horses. Lucky was a strong, fast horse. If only Lucky and I had been in Louisville that day and lined up for the Kentucky Derby, he would wear a blanket of roses, and we would be on to the next race in the Triple Crown.

Nothing like that goes through my mind at the time. I try to stay on Lucky. As a novice rider, this is a rough ride down the steep gravel road. Even worse, we approach hair-pin and switch-back curves, and Lucky does not slow down through them. Terrified. Can I stay on? Will Lucky fall at this break-neck speed down a steep incline, on loose gravel, and through these un-banked curves? Will we meet a car or truck? Mostly, I am just trying to stay on Lucky, "holding on for dear life." If stronger, I might break the horn off the saddle, holding it so tightly. Lucky and I streak past the other riders. Cousin Dennis often reminds me that as I went flashing by him I was screaming, "Whoa! Whoa! Whoa!"

At the bottom of the mountain on the first flat section of the road, Lucky slows to a trot. I pull up the reins. Lucky comes to a halt. A few minutes later, the riding crew with looks of disbelief and wonder reach the flat section of the road. They all want to know if I am okay? I am but still shaking inside. It is little comfort when my witty uncle says, "Dave, if you can stay on a horse after a ride like that, maybe you should go join the rodeo!" I appreciate once again I escape death and Reverend Leroy's haunting curse.

Since my father worked in the feldspar mines, I worried about his health for good reason. Feldspar workers often develop "white lung," as compared to "black lung" for coal miners. Medically it is silicosis. Feldspar comes out of the mines in large chunks and brought to the processing plant. The ore is dumped into a huge grinder that has steel teeth as large as a person and looks like something out of a science fiction movie. Crunching and grinding sounds deafen the ears. White dust billows into the air. Next the ground-up feldspar goes through various filtering systems and eventually bagged or blown into a railroad car. Eventually, the feldspar makes its way into white kitchen countertops or most often white bathroom fixtures (sinks, toilets).

Silicosis happens when a worker breaths in enough microscopic silica particles from the grinding, processing, or bagging of the feldspar to cut and injure the lungs. The average life span for a worker exposed to significant feldspar silica was about fifty. My grandfather, a life-long miner, Nate Boone, died from silicosis. I can still remember being at his house the night he dies. Like a sad family reunion, all thirteen adult children are there with spouses and children. Eight years old, I play outside with the other children. Occasionally, I come inside to get a glass of water. I hear the labored, heavy breathing of my grandfather in the next room. His breaths are like pinched squeals as his lungs beg for oxygen. He dies late that night when we are all in the house. His daughters cry and moan. His sons remained stoic. I'm traumatized having witnessed my first death. I was not that close to my grandfather, but I found the finality of death cold and shocking. Nathan Boone was not a Howell, so he had escaped the Hell-bound curse of Pastor Leroy.

The Howell and Boone families produce an incredible number of off-spring, almost crashing "23andMe" website. Grandparents have many children (thirteen on Boone side and twelve on Howell side) and grandchildren (fifty or more). One summer at a Howell family reunion, my grandfather as he points at me says, "Now, is that Jack's boy or Joe's boy? And what's his name?" My grandmother says, "That's Jack's boy, David." Grandmothers keep up with their grandchildren so much better than grandfathers.

I realize now I was angry at International Mineral and Chemical Corporation for having hazardous work conditions for my father and grandfather. A cold and uncaring company that didn't mind sending men to an early grave to generate profits. (On the other hand, there were not many jobs in the Appalachian Mountains. So there was that.) Kids at school taunt me a few times, "Your father works in the Kona silicosis mine!" as a stinging heat of embarrassment ripples across my face.

Surprising myself, I apply to work in the Kona silicosis mine one summer during college vacation and one Christmas vacation. Other jobs are available for college students in the area, but something compels me to work in the feldspar plant alongside my father. I still can't explain it. Maybe it is an effort to connect with him at some deeper level. Perhaps it is to identify with him as I work alongside him, filling bags with feldspar dust. We wear respirators most of the time, but not even the uneducated workers trusted them since they probably did not filter out microscopic particles. I worry about developing silicosis for many years and facing the curse, but so far it has not appeared.

As a child, anger boils in me over another mining company, although I did not call it anger at the time. Hours of psychotherapy helped me realize the anger. All the mining companies dump their byproducts into the rivers. So the once crystal clear mountain rivers (North Toe and South Toe Rivers) are an ugly opaque brown. The river that flows by our house should be clear and sparkling, full of fish and aquatic life. The ugly brown river moves like a mud-hole sliding down the mountain. The greedy mining companies ruined rivers and men's lives to make money.

The companies mining for feldspar and mica did not dig deep underground mines like the coal mines of West Virginia and Kentucky. In western North Carolina, they are "surface mines." In some cases, tops of mountains were literally removed, and the mining companies walked away leaving bare the mountains and slopes to erosion. It was an awful sight, ugly tones of light brown and light red with war-like craters. From our house, I could see the scalped mountains and in the air the glitter of small particles of silica and mica that had been blown into the air from the unconscionable mine processing plants. As a child I am furious.

Certainly, what I saw corporations do to their workers and to the rivers and land influenced my theology and core beliefs. The corporations clearly follow the economic theory espoused by economist Milton Friedman who contended that the sole responsibility of the corporation is to make a profit for its shareholders. This was before the Environmental Protection Agency. Corporations and our culture were still enjoying the unbridled economic hormonal rush of the industrial revolution. Fortunes were to be made, and the consequences to the environment would have to be dealt with down the road. Later I study reformed theology and the theology of Reinhold Niebuhr who insisted in his writings that humankind is essentially greedy, sinful, and left unchecked would pursue selfish ambitions while ignoring moral responsibilities. Then I read Carl Jung and his concept of the "shadow" in the human and communal psyche. It all made theological and practical sense to me.

One mountain top not scalped by the mining companies is at the head of Rebels Creek in Mitchell County. As a boy, I mistakenly think that Rebels Creek is named after a band of Confederate Rebels from the Civil War era. According to my historian brother, the babbling creek that winds its way from the top of the mountain through this isolated, narrow valley was named instead after a horse, Rebel. It is so disappointing in a young boy's mind when a romanticized piece of local lore is made so plainly common.

The Boones and Howells not settling in Boonford established their small farms and homes in Rebels Creek. The road up Rebels Creek twists and turns along the creek that is just barely too wide to jump across. A couple of miles up the creek are rare flat fields that were perfect for corn and bean crops while cattle could be raised on the cleared slopes of the mountains that rose up to the sky. Native Americans apparently cherished the area as well. According to my brother, when the valley ends where the soaring mountains halt all human advance, there are Native American hieroglyphics carved upon vertical rock formations.

The families scratching out an existence in this charming little valley, called Rebel's Creek, need a place to bury their dead. Life expectancy is abbreviated compared to today. Women die in childbirth. Children die in infancy due to a lack of vaccines. Young boys and men die in mining and farming accidents. Silicosis snatches older miners from their loved ones. Jealous lovers cannot control their rage upon being hurt and abandoned. Cemeteries are needed.

A famous jealous lover lived on the other side of the mountain from Rebels Creek. Since Rebels Creek is on a dead-end road, Kona is accessible only by NC 80 that continues to snake around the side of the mountain after the "exit" to Rebels Creek. The North Toe River roars about a half a mile straight down below the road. The road then stretches itself through a gap and down into the tiny village of Kona. Kona has one thing, Feldspar. K=potassium, O=oxygen, Na=sodium is the chemical makeup of feldspar. Kona is the name of the mine and the tiny community. A hundred-plus years later my father works at the Kona feldspar mine, but on December 22, 1831, a ghastly event in Kona shocks the neighbors and eventually the entire state.

Frances "Frankie" Silver, eighteen, and Charles "Johnny" Silver, nineteen, live as a legally married couple just off NC 80 as the road continues its journey to renowned places like Loafer's Glory, Bandana, and Buladean. Their daughter, Nancy, is thirteen months old. Does Johnny have a lover? Is Frankie murderously jealous? Or is Frankie the victim of domestic abuse (not at all uncommon in the mountains)? Whatever the reason, one evening after dark, Frankie fells Johnny with the blow of an ax. While the child sleeps, she cuts Johnny's body into little pieces as much as she can. The small pieces are burned in the fireplace. Deep snow falls outside. This part is not in the history books but was told to me as a child. Frankie puts on Johnny's boots and with his head and limbs in a sack over her shoulder walks down to the North Toe River. Using the same ax that killed Johnny, Frankie cuts a hole in the iced-over river and dumps the chunks of Johnny into the raging water. Frankie then walks backward in the same tracks to her cabin.

In the days ahead, Frankie swears Johnny got up in the middle of the night, walked to the river, and fell in. Johnny's family does not buy the story. When Frankie is away for part of a day, they ask a local hunter to go into the cabin and "have a look around." He finds fragments of human bones in greasy ashes in the fireplace and bloodstains underneath some of the floor planks.

My grandmother told us this story. It was a scary, spooky bedtime story. Grandma said her grandmother told her the same story and how she was outside her home the day the sheriff came up the road taking Frankie Silver to Morganton (county seat) in the back of a wagon pulled by two horses to jail and trial. Frankie was convicted of first-degree murder by an "all-male" jury. Strangely her lawyer advised her to plead innocent, instead of self-defense as a result of domestic abuse.

Led by prominent women in the Morganton community, a general sympathy for Frankie arises. Seven jurors sign a petition asking the governor for mercy. He refuses. Rumored to be an inside job, Frankie escapes. Dressed as a man, she is in the back of a wagon, covered in hay. Her liberators hope to get her to the Tennessee border. Sheriff Deputies though stop the wagon, and one asks the wagon driver,

"What's under the hay"?

"It's me, Tom." Frankie volunteers from under the hay.

"Yeah, her name is Tom." The driver goofs out.

Frankie is returned to Morganton. With noose around her neck, the hangman offers her "any final words?" Her father in the crowd gathered around the courthouse shouts "Die with it in ye Frankie!" Much speculation has gone on over the years about the father's words. Did she have help? What secret did Frankie die with?

The story of Frankie and Charles "Johnny" Silver will not go away. People continue to write articles arguing for her innocence due to self-defense. Senator Sam Irwin of Watergate fame and resident of Morganton shared his favorable opinion of Frankie's innocence. *The Ballad of Frankie Silver* is penned by Sharyn McCrumb. Frankie is featured in a television series called *Deadly Women*. Her segment is *Brides of Blood*. Frankie, justly or unjustly, hung to death, but at least she did not die under the curse of eternal Hell rendered by Reverend Leroy. Incidentally, Frankie's mother was a Howell, so maybe she did.[5]

Cougars and Decorations

"One lives in the hope of becoming a memory."
ANTONIO PORCHIA

MY GRANDMOTHER WAS ELSIE Jarratt Howell. The Jarratt family lived near Kona. One evening at her house before she died, she shares with my son and me a story that fascinated us. Talking about her childhood, she told us about walking home one evening from a friend's house. With a late start, it is dark, and she walks alone on the dirt country road. She hears something in the woods above her and then a "scream." The scream comes not from a person but from a panther (mountain lion, cougar).

Later that evening, Morgan, my son, asks me, "Are cougars still around here?"

"The biologists say they are extinct on the east coast, except in Florida, but some people here in the mountains still say they 'see' and 'hear' them." I answer.

"Let's find out." He says in his twelve-year old innocence.

"Let's do it!" I say out of my own childlike sense of adventure.

Soon, my son and I write to newspapers in the North Carolina and Virginia mountains asking them to publish a "blurb" for us in their newspapers. To my surprise, most agree! The blurb goes something like this: "Report Cougar Sightings: Call this number if you have seen a cougar, also called mountain lion or panther."

In a few weeks, our phone rings off the hook with reports of cougar sightings. Some are rubbish, probably pranksters. Some telling us that they have seen black panthers. Cougars in North America were never black. There are black jaguars in South America. Some of the calls are

90

hilariously ridiculous. One guy said he saw (probably after downing a fifth of moonshine) a white cougar chasing his girlfriend after they stopped on the side of the road for her to go to the bathroom in the woods.

Some of the called-in reports were believable (although no one ever offered any evidence). A young man riding his bike on the Blue Ridge Parkway sees a large cat-like animal running across the road in front of him. He does not think much about it until he sees a cougar in a zoo with a sign saying that they now only reside in Florida and the western states. A farmer living high in the mountains says he has lost several cattle to cougars and his horse had a large bite on his neck that the veterinarian said could come only from a large animal (cougars attack the back of the neck).

Many phone calls came in from people living in an area between Yellow Mountain, Tennessee, and Brown Mountain, North Carolina. So many calls, we named it "The Cougar Corridor." It is a rugged mountain area. The headwaters of the Toe and Linville rivers are in the area, along with the famed Linville Gorge.

A man calls. In the conversation, I discover that he works for my uncle. The man reports several sightings in the "cougar corridor." After our conversation, I call my uncle and ask him if this man is believable. He assures me that he is.

My son and I venture on after dark reconnaissance missions on the Blue Ridge Parkway. One mission took us to Mount Pisgah on the Blue Ridge Parkway. Our basecamp is the Mt. Pisgah Inn. After dinner, we drive miles up and down the parkway in this rugged area. A long shot, we hope to see a cougar crossing the parkway. I start driving back to the inn after a fruitless night of driving. I notice my son has fallen asleep in the passenger seat. We are crossing over Mount Pisgah. The road is very crooked. We come around a turn and on the side of the road is a large furry brown animal with long legs. Adrenaline rushes through my body. "Morgan!" I scream. "Wake up, cougar!" The animal starts to run up the road before turning into the forest. At the last moment, the animal looks back at us. We see a snicker-like grin on the face. It is a coyote.

No one ever produced any physical evidence of the existence of a cougar, although many farmers and ranchers living in the higher elevations of Western North Carolina insist on their existence. Mount Mitchell, the highest mountain east of the Rockies, is in Western North Carolina with lots of rugged forests in the area. My brother and others were amused by our research project. I was the butt of several funny jokes, as they compared me to one of the *Ghostbusters*. My son gets an opportunity to play baseball, and we abandon the project (although a professor at a college reportedly picked up the research project). When my brother teased me about abandoning the quest, I told him that we were going to start "alien research."

Cemeteries embed themselves as an often necessary part of mountain life. The early pioneers establish "Rebels Creek Cemetery" near the headwaters of the creek. The burial ground sits on a mountain flat-top with lush green fields below. In the distance the majestic, rugged peaks of Celo Knob and Mount Mitchell (highest point east of the Rockies) tower to the sky. Mountain people and southern folks had traditions that helped them remember and honor their dead. One of the great traditions of southern culture is Decoration Sunday.

Decoration Sunday originated during the Civil War as women brought flowers to husbands' or others' graves. Many argue, though, that the tradition goes back to the days of the early settlers. Pioneers' lives were extremely hard. Death often came early in life, and the living sought to honor the memories of the dead. It is also rightly pointed out that this southern, mountain tradition inspired the declaration of a national Memorial Day in 1971.

For Rebels Creek Cemetery, families celebrate Decoration Sunday on the fourth Sunday in July. The quiet little community starts changing early in the week. Local families gather at the cemetery for the annual "big clean-up." Fallen grave markers and tilting tombstones uprighted. Grass cut, weeds pulled. The steep road up to the cemetery has potholes and gullies in need of repair. The fence around the cemetery is mended, boards re-nailed and painted. Finally, the stage is set for the biggest event of the year in the southern Appalachian Mountains.

Family members who moved to places like Atlanta and Charlotte to "make a living" start arriving. On Friday evening, surviving family members place gorgeous wreaths and vases of gladioli, red poppies, peach roses, purple iris, snapdragons, dahlias, marigolds, zinnias, and local yellow daisies on the graves.

By Saturday afternoon, driveways up and down Rebels Creek, even front yards, fill with cars, some with Georgia, Tennessee, South Carolina license plates. Some relatives have "hit it big" in the cities of Charlotte and Atlanta. Their spotless Cadillacs and big Buicks sit quietly and proudly beside old farm trucks and dilapidated cars driven by less fortunate kinfolks who stayed in the mountains. Children who only see each other once a year are chasing each other across freshly mown green "yards" (only recently in the mountains are "yards" called "lawns"). Porch swings never get a break as family members take turns kicking their feet high in the air.

Saturday dinners are banquet-like but are surpassed by the true feast of the Sunday mid-afternoon meal when cultures come together. On long tables for self-serving sit our humble vittles of pork chops with sawmill gravy, sliced country ham, infamous chitlins, fried chicken, chicken livers and gizzards, corn on the cob, green beans cooked with large ham hocks, cat-head biscuits, fresh-picked blackberries, and fried homemade apple pies. Successful relatives now living in places like Atlanta or Charlotte bring foods to share that we have never seen before. Our well-to-do aunts and uncles from the cities place bowls of boiled Georgia shrimp (children are not allowed to eat), fried green tomatoes, sweet Vidalia onions, peach cobbler, watermelons, and jugs of tea so sweet one glass puts a cavity in a soft enamel tooth. Some years, such a bounty of food exists on this day that some bowls sit on the ground until space on the table becomes available.

Sunday morning witnesses a once-a-year preparation. The finest clothes go on. Women adorn themselves in colorful, bright dresses, and boastful hats. This might be the only time during the year that some of the men put on "a suit of clothes" and a necktie, although they complain about the unnaturalness of it all. This is one of the few days in the mountains that people can dress up and not be accused of "puttin on airs" ("airs of superiority") which meant you were trying to be "someone you ain't."

People arrive early on this holiest of days to be part of this command performance at the graves of the dead. Some arrive by 9:00 AM "to visit" the dead and see relatives "from off somewhere." Hands shake, hugs are given, and tears roll down cheeks. The hot sun causes sweat to run down foreheads, chests, and backbones, but there is no other place to be. Suddenly without introduction, a gospel choir starts singing in one corner of the cemetery. Soon they will lead the entire gathering in rounds of "I'll Fly Away", "In the Sweet By and By", and "When We All Get To Heaven." Then the pastor of Rebels Creek Baptist Church reads scripture and still holding the Bible in his raised hand begins to warn the unsaved among the crowd of the perils of Hell. He chides the people who are now living in cities that he says are like modern-day Sodoms and Gomorrahs and cautions them to stay away from these "dens of inequities." Ironically, in the early 1980s, a young man after attending college went to a big city to work, and early in the AIDS crisis he dies. The locals permit him to be buried at Rebels Creek cemetery but outside the fence. His grave and marker are all alone on the other side of the rear parking lot.

The preacher clearly believes some listening to his words will experience an eternal punishment much more blistering and painful than this morning sun shining intensely upon the mountain top. As a young man, sermons about eternal life on Decoration Sundays and at other times confuse me. This preacher talks about going to Heaven in the blink of an eye, like the thief on the cross beside Jesus, "Today, you will be with me in paradise." In a sermon in another time and setting, a different preacher explains that the dead rest in their graves until Resurrection Day, which usually includes a Judgment Day. Souls who have "been saved" in their earthly lives come out of their graves and get to proceed through the "Pearly Gates," "walk the streets paved with gold," and rejoice with long-departed loved ones. So which is it? Immediate entrance to Heaven for the saved upon death? Or rest in the grave until Resurrection Day?

Perplexed for many years, I decided at one of those Decoration Sundays it does not matter for one small group of earthly creatures. No dilemma exists for the Howells resting in their graves on the top of that mountain. Their poor wretched souls are already condemned to eternal, fiery Hell with no chance of Heaven's glories.

"Who's Next to Die?"

*"Sometimes the people with the
worst past create the best future . . ."*
UMAR IBN AL-KHATTAB

DEATH STOKES MY ANXIETY several times during high school. I sit beside
Bryan Bishop in every class. We don't socialize outside class, but we talk
at every opportunity. Although we are in the same class, he is two years
older, as are all my classmates. Bryan is the starting point guard on the
basketball team, the quarterback on the football team, and gets elected
to escort the homecoming queen at half-time. Every young woman in
school wants to date him. He has "a steady girlfriend," but his parents
think they are getting too serious.

Arriving at school on a Monday morning in March, the halls stay
unusually quiet. Something has happened. Young women cry. Guys normally laughing and joking are straight-faced and serious. The evening
before Bryan wants to use the family car and go see his girlfriend. His
parents say he should stay home and that he is getting too serious about
this young woman. Bryan goes upstairs to his bedroom. His family hunts,
and he has several guns. He comes out of his room to the top of the steps,
puts the shotgun under his chin, and pulls the trigger.

Shocked for a few days, we adjust to Bryan's deadly impulsive behavior. The month of May brings warmer temperatures and warmer water to
the deep swirling waters on Celo Creek, which is big and deep enough
that it should have been name Celo River. Another classmate Johnny
Jones swims one Sunday afternoon, cramps, and never comes out of the
water alive. We are stunned by death once again.

The following winter Bryan Bishop's best friend, Stanley Bailey, after an evening at the movies (also called the "picture show"), drops his girlfriend off at her house in Burnsville. Driving too fast on NC 80, his car leaves the road and rolls down an embankment, stopping a few feet short of the South Toe River. He's not dead, only because the cold temperatures keep him from bleeding to death, but in a coma for over two months. When he finally emerges from the coma, he lost so much weight he hardly looks like the same person. Before the accident, he was outspoken, loud, sometimes obnoxious. Now, he is subdued and quiet. About nine months later, Stanley once again drives late at night on the same road, and eerily, runs off the road in about the same place and is pronounced dead at the scene.

The guys and I begin to wonder: Who's next?

My other best friend in high school did not die, but it was still a loss for me.

Brandon tells me one day, "I'm quittin' school."

"Why? Why would you do that?" I demand.

"Goin' to pedal fruits and vegetables up on Three Mile Ridge. There's a real good spot on the side of the road for a vegetable-stand up there now, and I better grab it before someone else does."

With a lot of denial and repression (the two most basic and primitive psychological defense mechanisms according to Freud), I soon put the loss, death anxiety, and the theological questions of God's judgment in my rearview mirror. The hormones of adolescence overcome the concerns of eternal damnation. At sixteen, with keys to my own car that did run most of the time, I become an existentialist. Not that I read Jean-Paul Sartre or Albert Camus, but I live for the moment. Turning sixteen in my senior year in high school and after watching my friends drive and socialize since our sophomore years, I have some social catching up to do. Life is like a wild joy ride in a stolen car. At the same time, I am driven to excel scholastically, determined that poverty and social disadvantage will not define me.

On course to finish in the top three academically of my high school senior class, I am accepted at several universities. I want to attend the University of North Carolina at Chapel Hill. After proudly declaring to all my friends my intentions, I receive a crushing blow. My parents decided that I am too young to attend a large university because I will be "corrupted." The college my parents choose for me is closer to home and much smaller. I reluctantly accept the change of course. Even then, I deeply appreciate the difficulty and sacrifice my parents make to send now the third of three children to college on minimum wage jobs. There are probably scholarships available, but no one brings them to my awareness.

Late August and the day before I depart for college, the car is packed. My future seems wide open with endless possibilities. College, a whole new world to explore, awaits me. The evening before my departure, my father comes to me and says, "You won't be gone long. You'll never make it in college. You'll be back here soon." It is a blow with an emotional baseball bat. I can't believe my ears. I will not believe my ears! Briefly stunned, I resolve to push ahead. College here I come. I resolved in those moments that I will not "be back here soon." Johnny Cash first recorded Shel Silverstein's "A Boy Named Sue" on February 24, 1969. My father tried to label me as "A Boy Named Failure" in August of 1968. Both, I suppose, were paradoxical blessings. Sue was ridiculed for his name and learned to fight and emerged tough as nails.

College life blossoms as one "wow" experience after another. The dorm is like an anthropological zoo to this naïve sixteen-year old mountain lad. The students are from everywhere: big cities, small towns, different states (even Florida, guys talked about surfing a few days before . . . while I had yet to see the ocean). Wide-eyed, I take it all in and marvel at the diversity. There are four of us for two sets of bunk beds in our dorm room. Two of the guys are high school friends from Raleigh and announce they have no intention of staying in college past the first semester. College is their parents' ideas. They are not going to class, so they can "flunk out" and be back in their hometown for good by Christmas because this campus is so boring. They miss their friends and good times back home.

Boring? How could they think this place is boring? The campus buzzes with excitement. Fraternities, sororities, and a campus to my experience has a multitude of things to do. Although I adapt quickly, I am more out of place than I even realize. At sixteen, I am the youngest person on campus. I am from a place no one has ever heard of Boonford, North Carolina. I've never been in a large city, let alone another state.

If several of us are hanging out in a dorm room, relaxing, and if I have a cola or a soft drink, I might offer it to anyone in the room as we did in Boonford. "Anyone want a 'sup'?" Or if I had a candy bar, anyone want a "bite?" Hilarious, the guys think. I explain that my mother taught me that if I had something good it should be shared.

It is good-natured fun, and I go along with it (in an effort to gain acceptance), but occasionally the guys on the hall gather in one of the larger rooms and ask me to say certain words. "David say 'pipe' for us." I do, and they erupt in laughter. "David say 'air'" (the way I say "air" sounds like "hair"). I do and more laughter. Like everyone else in the hollows and little valleys around Boonford, I pronounced some words differently from these city boys "from off somewhere" like Atlanta or St Petersburg, Florida. But it is all in good fun. I belong.

Not all the guys hail from big cities. Vern Bailey, one of the four in our dorm room, is from the little town of Murphy, North Carolina. Murphy is tucked away in the Great Smoky Mountains in far western North Carolina. Vern's family are tobacco farmers. In that part of North Carolina, farmers grow burley tobacco that is harvested in the Fall. Vern's first loyalty is to his family and to their tobacco crop. About 4:00 AM one October Wednesday morning, Vern's alarm clock rings. It wakes us all up. We can't believe it. We never get up before seven o'clock, if not later. Vern is dressed in an instant. A phone call the night before alerts him to something he must attend to back home. "Baccer is in case, boys. I gotta go home and help." Out the door, he goes. We learn later that "baccer in case" means that the family's tobacco crop is ready to be harvested, cut off at the ground, and hung upside down in tobacco barns to dry and cure.

Plenty apprehensive about college courses, I dread the possibility of going home a failure and fulfill my father's curse (as you will see later I get the same curse again as a post-graduate professional). I go to class. I study. I can do this. I go home for Christmas with my name on The Dean's List, 3.6 GPA. I don't recall a reaction from my father since he was not one to show emotion. I think he was proud.

Unlike most of the guys in the dorm, my parents didn't give me "spending money." Somehow, they raked enough money together to pay my tuition, but it was up to me to work summers, Christmas vacations, and part-time jobs at college to have that much-needed spending money. So that first Christmas vacation is spent in the feldspar plant, loading boxcars. A lot of the guys in the dorm are back in Florida surfing or enjoying the social life of the Atlanta suburbs.

Back at college for the second semester, the fraternities come calling. They like my GPA, and I guess figure I will grow out of my social and cultural immaturity. The college rule is no one could "pledge" a fraternity the first semester. But a student with at least a 2.0 could go through the "pledging process" and by the middle of the second semester be a fraternity man. There are two "cool" fraternities on campus. One invites me to their "rush party," where academically qualified and invited freshmen meet "the brothers" and their women, all stunningly attractive to my eyes. George Lucas has not yet filmed *Star Wars*, but it is like stepping into Mos Eisley Cantina the first time I step through the door and into that fraternity party scene. Strong drinks, hot loud tunes, and sexy women are in abundance in the Mardi Gras-like scene.

I pledge the fraternity. Pledging is a six-week process consisting of passing a test on fraternity history, by-laws, etc., and enduring a series of projects requiring each "brothers'" signature. Polishing shoes, washing a car, picking up laundry get a signature. The pledging class has weekend group projects. The frat brothers borrow a church basement. We are blindfolded and driven to the church just after dark. Led into the basement we are seated on the floor and ordered not to speak. We sit there for hours in silence and darkness. It is 4:00 AM when we are led out of the church basement and get our signatures for keeping the silence. The brothers say they need to know we can keep our mouths shut before we learn the well-kept secrets of the fraternity.

Another Saturday morning a fraternity brother goes on a wooded hillside and drives nails into the base of a dozen trees. Late afternoon and just as massive clouds release snowflakes to float to earth, we are driven to the hillside, given crowbars and flashlights for pulling out the nails once we find them, and told not to come out of the woods until we could come out with all twelve nails. Snow falls heavily from the pregnant bellies of the clouds and is now over ten inches deep. Winds pick up, and snow blows sideways. After two hours of digging snow away from the base of trees, we find only three nails. It seems impossible, and it is. One of the pledges is also a football player, a massive offensive tackle. I am a wee lad of sixteen and not even physically mature. I figure I will endure the cold and the pain but not footballer James "Big Man" Tucker. "Goddamn-it, I'm cold!" Big Man roars as he throws his crowbar through the air. Luckily the crowbar strikes a tree and not one of the pledges or one of the two supervising fraternity brothers (who quickly huddle and announce it is time to leave).

One of the fraternity brothers shines as the star of the college tennis team. His father is president of a bank in Charlotte, NC. My frat brother, Charles A. Mullins III, has spent his life at the high-priced Myers Park country club. His golf game is outstanding, but he excels at tennis. I need his signature and contract with him to wash his car at his convenience, but I tend to be an impatient sort. It is a warm, pleasant spring Saturday afternoon when the college tennis team hosts the finals of the conference championship. I have never been to a tennis court before. Boonford is fifty miles from the nearest court.

When we arrive at the court, Charlie is deep into the conference championship match and losing badly. He is not happy as he is not accustomed to losing. It just happens I am standing near the fence and not far from where Charlie prepares to serve. He bounces the tennis ball a couple of times on the court, eyes the net, and prepares to toss the ball into the air for his serve when I decide it is a good time to ask, "Charlie, can I wash your car this afternoon?" Instantly, I knew. Charlie is stunned. People around me gasp. I feel the shame. My face glows brighter than the sun with embarrassment. Amazingly, the blatant social gaff is never mentioned to me. I figure I will be shown the fraternity door and asked to never return. I suppose the guys knew I have a bit of social learning curve.

Each pledge has an "older brother," one of the established members of the fraternity that guides the new recruit through the gauntlet of pledging. My older brother is Bobby. He could have been a good influence on me, but I am not ready. Bobby is the most mature of all the fraternity brothers. He attends church and teaches Sunday School. He parties and drinks but never to excess. He is admired by all.

A fateful Friday afternoon arrives as Bobby's turn to make the drive to a neighboring town about forty miles away to get the weekend liquor for the fraternity's Friday and Saturday evening parties. Bobby is a senior and twenty-two years old so he can purchase liquor. I am invited to take the drive with Bobby. My Friday afternoon class runs late. Bobby, Fred, and Bill leave without me. Not a big deal. They are on a mission, procure liquor for the Friday evening party.

On the way home, Bobby loses control of the car. The car flips, and all three passengers are thrown from the car (no one is wearing a seat belt). Fred and Bill are young, flexible, and fine, even after taking the unintended flight. Bobby's head hits a rock, and he is pronounced dead on the scene. It is a sad weekend at the fraternity house, but the parties go on. No surprise there.

Why Bobby? We wonder. He was the best of us. The lone church attendee. A Sunday School teacher. Relative to other college students, he was living the Christian life. It is a theological head-scratcher. One of the fraternity brothers offers an explanation: He was ready. We were not. The theory is accepted, and we put it behind us.

If I arrived at the meeting place a few minutes earlier, I would have been in that car that flipped through the air. Would I have survived like Fred and Bill? Or would I have suffered the same fate as Bobby? It had been a long time since I had considered Pastor Leroy's curse. It gave me pause but not for long.

A war rages, but I only have a passing interest. I often walk by the tv room at the fraternity house, coming in from class or work, in the early evening. Either Chet Huntley or David Brinkley give the body counts for the day: seven-hundred and eighty-six Viet Cong and North Vietnamese regulars and thirty-six United States soldiers. Every day's report is similar. We are obviously winning, and they will surrender, I thought. But the war is not being won. We are losing the war at home for the support of the conflict in far-away Southeast Asia. Volunteerism is much less popular. The military lottery is started.

The defense department issues the first lottery numbers for the Vietnam War Draft. On that fateful evening, we watch television as lottery numbers are assigned. College deferments are over. One of my good friends gets seven. He is going to Vietnam. He cries like a baby. Another friend gets three-hundred. He starts drinking beer and celebrates his good fortune.

I receive 170. The year before the military takes everyone through 200 if they pass a physical. But the war is winding down and that year they only take through 160. Close call . . . Pastor Leroy.

The counter-culture movement expands. More guys grow long hair and beards. Young women display their bell-bottomed jeans. There are "alternatives" suddenly available to beer and liquor. One afternoon after class, one of the fraternity brothers secretly confides in me, "I can't wait. I'm going to drop acid tonight." He did or at least he said he did. It did not seem to change him, but dropping acid did not appeal to me. I don't like the thought of losing control. Another friend warned "when you drop, you are going to see yourself as other people see you . . . be ready for that." Uh, no thanks. But I did like the hippie movement. I grew my hair longer and dressed differently. When home, my father's worse nightmare seems to be coming true. His son is a hippie! Not really a hippie, simply growing longer hair and wearing tye-dyed shirts. He starts to understand.

Summer comes. I accidentally receive a big introduction to hippie and anti-war culture. I work that summer at a local hosiery mill, a "runner," keeping the sewing machine operators in supplies. A New England company planted a garment factory in Spruce Pine (there were several of them around, cheap labor "in 'em thar hills"). I leave work that Friday afternoon and on the way home stop at my friend Larry's gas station. His father owns the station, but Larry operates it during the summer while his father farms and speculates in real estate.

I stop to kill some time. Unlike most weekends, I have no plans. "Wanna to go to a big music event with me?" Larry asks. Figuring it is not too far away and with nothing else on the social calendar, I shrug my shoulders, "Sure, let me go home and throw some clothes in a bag."

About an hour later, I return to the gas station, and Larry is ready to go. "First, we have to go to Asheville and meet up with some of my friends at my apartment." He says. Larry is a student at UNC-Asheville and shares an apartment with some guys. They scrape some money together and buy a real old school bus, but they can't get it running. Larry grew up working on engines. He has it running like a top by 1:00 AM.

Woodstock was held earlier that summer; so, I know we aren't going there. What I find out is that we are headed to Love Valley, a farm outside Charlotte, NC, where indeed there is going to be a Woodstock-like music festival.

By the time all the festival-goers arrive and board the bus, it is 2:00 AM, but we only have a four hour trip to Love Valley. A car could do it in three, but the old bus is turtle slow. We won't get a ticket for speeding but maybe for "faulty equipment" or "lack of proper something."

We arrive in the Love Valley vicinity at around 6:00 AM. Two-hundred thousand people are already there, not a Woodstock crowd of 400,000 but still a lot more people than in Boonford. An old, narrow, dirt, one-lane, farm road wiggles its way through a large grassy field to the newly built stage nestled in a wide ravine with perfectly sloped hills on three sides for amphitheater-like seating. Cars are parked on each side of the road. The bus barely squeezes through as we peel off car mirrors and door handles on each side of the road.

We approach an intersection. One way leads to overflow parking. The other way leads to the stage area. Festival traffic directors point all cars toward the overflow parking. The bus cannot make the sharp turn to overflow parking. The traffic guru barked unhappily, "Go on and park up by the stage. You're too damn big!"

The impressive music line-up includes original members of The Allman Brothers Band: Duane Allman and Gregg Allman. Additional musicians included Radar, Peace Core, Freedom 70, and a lot of regional bands to belt-out hard rock over the three-day event. A rumor floats that

Janis Joplin's band, Big Brother and the Holding Company, is coming. So an expectation already exists when a few early risers emerge from their tents and some who are sleeping on the ground see a bus headed toward the bus parking lot where the other musician buses are parked. Like a wildfire, word spreads that it is Big Brother and the Holding Company. Thousands, it seems, are running toward our bus chanting "Big Brother! Big Brother!"

We find a parking place for the old bus. Larry wants us to get on top of the bus and sing "Down on Me." We are afraid of what might happen if the masses find out we are imposters. Then we start to break the bad news to the hopeful gathered around our bus that we are not Big Brother, just a bunch of college students who barely get a bus to run long enough to get there. Disappointment is on their faces, but as we soon find out, most have something for their pain.

Loud hard rock music starts early. Speakers boom. The crowd cheers. Guitars pierce the air with their riveting chords. The crowd roars in approval. The air is thick with a sweet, pleasing smoke (not from campfires).

I possess no advanced knowledge or expectation of this event, but everyone seems to be having a great time. "Where have all these hippies come from?" I wonder. "Up north," someone says. Made sense to me.

Friends of a guy on the bus arrive. They drive to the event and make the trek from overflow parking. He looks exactly like the actor Elliott Gould who recently starred in the wildly successful *Love Story*. Monica with him is attractive but subdued, shy. After a time of conversation, "Elliott" pulls out a short rubber hose and wraps it around her arm. Then he pulls out a syringe and gives her an injection. With the same cool precision, he performs the same procedure on himself. I whisper to Larry, "Interesting they're both diabetics and have those insulin injections." Larry roars with laughter, "Heroin!" Elliott and Monica float in intense pleasure.

We enjoy the music and the crowd. A woman in the crowd becomes so musically and drug enthralled she takes off her top. Already bra-less, she gives her upper anatomy to the adorning crowd.

The air radiates hot. The music beats on, and the crowd responds in approval. A few tempers flare. Two young men exchange blows in the midst of the crowd. The music stops and 200,000 people chant: "Love! Love! Love!" Soon, they realize everyone's gaze is fixed upon them, and the fight is over. "Love is all you need," I guess.

Illegal drugs pass around. Some partake. I am afraid, the old fear of losing control. What if I "trip" and in my altered consciousness, Reverend

Leroy with his massive head of jet black hair and bushy eyebrows appears on the stage interrupting the music and declaring, "If any Howells are here, just know you are going to Hell!"

I stay clean, probably drank beer, I can't remember. Late afternoon, word spreads in our group we are going swimming in a nearby pond. "I don't have a swimsuit," I protest. Everybody laughs, and one young woman says, "Come on. You won't need one." At the pond, everyone, male and female, takes off clothes and jumps in the water. It is a crash course in sex education.

Beach Boys!

"Experience is the teacher of all things . . ."

JULIUS CAESAR

THE NEXT SUMMER, STILL sixteen, I am determined to see the ocean. Our neighbors go every summer, but our family has never been. When I ask my parents about our vacation limitations, my mother always has the same explanation, "We'll go next year." My father is a bit more philosophical. He points out he has worked hard, saved, and built large parts of our house in his spare time. And now why should he leave that hard-worked-for house to go to another house and pay them to stay there? Don't tell Airbnb, but that makes a lot of sense. My mother has another logical explanation some of the time: "It's cool here in the mountains. Why would we want to go off to the beach and burn-up in the hot sun?" Yes, and probably save on dermatologists' bills as well.

My friend Larry and I plan a summer beach trip. We ask mutual friends Greg and Jerry to go with us. Larry wants to drive, taking his trailer and motorcycle. We all agree and soon head to Myrtle Beach. We set up a tent in a family campground. Hot summer, sweat runs into the eyes and down the back. The campground is nearly full. Families and their tents are all around us, at least for the first few days. We stay out late at night, return well after midnight, and make a bounty of noise in the campground when all the families are trying to sleep. In a couple of days, all the camp sites around us are vacant as the families move to other sites in the campground as far away from us as possible.

I dive into the ocean for the first time. Yeah, I can see why people come here and "burn up." It's fun on the beach. The ocean is so vast, and later as I learn from Carl Jung "the ocean is a symbol of our unconscious-ness . . . deep and mysterious . . ."

We paid for a week at the campground. The week ends on Saturday, but four mountain boys tire of the heat. The guys start talking about leav-ing early. We've had lots of fun. I've seen the ocean for the first time, but goodness it is hot. No relief comes for us, except for the slightly milder temperatures at night.

On Thursday morning, the heat of the morning sun chases us out of our tent. Where is Larry? He is nowhere around, and his motorcycle is gone. We fire up the Coleman stove and fix breakfast of crispy bacon and scrambled eggs. We ate Larry's eggs and bacon too because we start talking about the possibility Larry is on his motorcycle and headed home. He was the one most eager to leave.

By mid-morning, we decide to take down the tent and pack up in case Larry has indeed gone home. Maybe he didn't want to wake us? Maybe he forgot to tell us he was headed back to the mountains?

Down to the beach, Larry is not to be found. Puzzled and scratch-ing our heads, we come back to the campground, pack up, and head to the Pavilion area of Myrtle Beach to look for Larry. The Pavilion area is decorated with Ferris-wheels and rotating swing rides filled with scream-ing teenagers. We agreed if he isn't there he is certainly "headed home."

We see no sign of Larry at the pavilion/amusement area. We're mountain bound, certain that Larry is hours ahead of us and probably getting close to home by now.

Almost dark, we arrive at Larry's small mountain family-farm (they all tend to be small since flat land is rare). We are in Larry's car and pull-ing Larry's trailer, but we don't have Larry or his motorcycle. We step out of the vehicle, innocently expecting Larry to walk out of the house at any second. Instead, Larry's father thunders out the door, his face red hot with anger. "You boys left Larry at the beach. He's down there with nothing but shorts, a t-shirt, and two quarters!"

Larry met a girl the day before and without telling us arranged an early morning rendezvous with her. He did not want us to know about the young woman because he was in a long-term relationship with a young woman back home. When Larry returned to the campground that day, he must have been shocked that we were gone. He had two quarters in his pocket. He used one quarter to call his father and explain his plight. The other quarter he used for gas for his motorcycle to get him part of the way home. He told people (he would not speak to us for weeks) that he would stop at small gas stations as he wound his way through the Carolinas, explain his dilemma, and ask for a gallon or two of free gas. He arrived home at 2:00 AM. With only a t-shirt and shorts, he was severely sunburned from the day of riding in the sun.

Larry's father calls all our parents, outraged at what we had done. We also hear Larry's father brings this up at the Board of Deacons meeting at Born Again Church. Larry's father is not only on the Board but close friends with Pastor Leroy. Pastor Leroy probably revels in a Howell involvement in what is perceived as another shenanigan. Certainly, more evidence that Howells are destined for fiery Hell.

When I return home that summer from my first dip in the ocean, I learn things heat up for Pastor Leroy at Born Again Church. His preaching is powerful, convincing. His personality is magnetic but trouble is brewing. Once a month, he schedules a baptism for new converts. Earl Tipton has a pond on his farm perfect for baptisms with an abundance of parking in the fields. The water stays shallow for thirty feet before getting dangerously deep. The baptisms for the usual two or three converts are held on Sunday afternoons. After morning services and a Sunday church dinner on the grounds, church members follow Leroy and the converts to Earl Tipton's farm. Pastor Leroy in a white robe enters the water first. He quotes scripture. Then each convert one by one, also in a white robe, is invited to "come into the waters." Leroy asks them several questions, including if they have truly repented of their sins and if they are ready to be reborn? "You will die in these waters and arise a new person, cleansed of your sins!" Quoting more scripture, he puts both arms under them and lowers them into water. After they are fully submerged, Leroy declares that this man or woman is dead and a new man or woman will now emerge from the waters. The faithful gathered on the banks roar with approval and applause as the man or woman, gasping, and often spewing water, is lifted from the pond by the beaming Pastor.

One Sunday afternoon, an abundant harvest awaits Pastor Leroy as he has six converts ready for the saving waters of Earl Tipton's pond. It is a family of two parents and four children. The younger, terrified children are baptized first. As usual, everything centers around Pastor Leroy. Even though a series of dark storm clouds are approaching, each baptism is like a King's coronation, although Leroy is the obvious King. Thunder soon rumbles. Leroy has only baptized two children. Light rain starts to fall as Leroy finishes the last child. The congregation is increasingly nervous as thunder booms all around them, and lightning bolts fill the sky.

Some of the faithful start to leave. Pastor Leroy will have none of it. "Don't be weak! Stay for the Lord's work! The Lord will protect us! We are his chosen!" Husbands and wives look at each other, and the looks on their faces show they are sorely afraid. Leroy becomes firmer and threatens them, "You are being tested. If you leave now, the Lord knows you are not a true believer!" Sheepishly, they return to the pond's bank. The sky is alive with nature's electricity. Pastor Leroy shouts to speak over the loud claps of thunder. He takes his time and baptizes the two adults. He then declares the Lord's work is done and praises his followers for their steadfastness. He points out to them that indeed the Lord protected them, the storm passed, and not one hair on their heads was harmed. Pastor Leroy masterfully uses biblical imagery.

Church members begin to whisper among themselves that perhaps Pastor Leroy is some kind of prophet with a special relationship with God. Enhancing his mystique is he does not have any family. He comes to the area to work originally in the hosiery plant. When asked about his family, he quickly and dismissively says, "I don't have any." He is mysterious. He lives alone with window shades always drawn. The church and his control of the church is his life. When he walks down the streets of the little towns of Burnsville and Spruce Pine, people whisper among themselves, "That's him, the pastor of Born Again Church who baptizes people with water and lightning." Pastor Leroy's narcissism enjoys the extra attention and flattery.

With Pastor Leroy and his curse temporarily out of my mind, I resume college in September. None of my fraternity brothers worry about salvation or any kind of faith matters. We do our academic work, some just enough to get by, and have our parties.

My narcissism causes me to conduct an experiment for the semester. I want to impress my fraternity brothers any way I can. Low self-esteem and narcissism often go hand in hand (co-morbidity). I calculate I can impress my fraternity brothers if I do not go to class all semester and still make good grades. After attending the first class of each course to get the syllabus, I spend my days in the local college cafe where we listen to Grand Funk Railroad, Jimi Hendrix, The Doors, and Crosby, Stills, Nash, and Young. I work several hours per day in the billiards hall of the student center. I still study for tests, usually mid-terms and final exams.

I also discover an underground group of guys who don't go to class, nor do they study. They are academic burglars living on the edge of crime. Taking the same classes, they figure out ways to gain late-night entry into the buildings housing the offices of the professors of the courses. For one building, maybe they find a window on a lower level that is never locked, and for another building a back door that can be pried open with a screwdriver. After they locate the professor offices (most left unlocked), they go on nocturnal missions to swipe a copy of the upcoming mid-term or final test. I have way too much anxiety to go with them on their mid-night escapades, but I do benefit from some of the stolen tests. They cannot break into every building or office. Some have all their windows locked and their doors are secure. So the guys solely dependent on the stolen tests have a hard time passing those courses. My grades suffered that semester. I didn't impress anyone.

In the spring, our attention turns to the beach once again. The fraternity brothers who are much more traveled than I am talk about how much fun the Ocean Drive section of North Myrtle Beach is. My previous summer's trip to Myrtle Beach was to South Myrtle Beach. So on a Friday morning in early May four of us skip Friday classes and head "to the beach."

Joey offers to drive his car. It is a six-hour drive. I ride "shotgun." We stop for a lunch of vinegar-based barbeque sandwiches and french-fries smothered in bright red catsup. The drive-in restaurant has a server on roller skates who skates out to our car with the food. The skating server is a young woman squeezed into a skimpy short white dress, an extra serving of bright red lipstick on her naturally puckered lips and short curly blonde hair. Joey thinks she likes him. We laugh and tell him that she is just looking to enhance her tip.

Bill and Fred in the backseat ask Joey to stop for beer. Joey insists he cannot drink and drive, and I offer to abstain in case Joey needs a relief driver. We stop at a beer joint off the two-lane road. An oval ESSO sign and a bright Nehi Big Orange sign welcome us. A couple of guys in faded denim overalls sit on wooden drink crates in front of the store. An overweight young guy with glistening auburn hair squats beside them as they all drink cheap Thunderbird red wine from the same bottle. They let out a good snicker at the college boys going back to the car with their booze. Do they know what is in store for us?

The guys in the backseat start feeling "real good" after a few beers, and they share stories of their fun times at The Barrel, The Pad, and the Swinging Medallion in Ocean Drive. These are all clubs for college students, all situated on an intersection near the beach with each located on a corner of the intersection. Students from colleges and universities all over North and South Carolina taking a weekend get-away from the college campuses drink, mingle, and dance until the wee hours of the morning, often moving from one club to another.

When we arrive at the parking lot on the fourth corner of the intersection, we are ready to unwind from the long trip. Music blasts from each venue, laughter roars above the music sometimes. As I get out of the car, my eyes are big with anticipation. Wow, it looks to be everything the guys said it was. All at once, an already intoxicated Fred who has stepped out of the car screams as loud as a human can scream, "Holy Shit! We're here! Let's party!"

A different destination and experience, not a party, awaits Fred. From around the corner of a building, two uniformed police officers are bearing down on us. "Looks like you boys had too much to drink," we are shocked to hear from the first officer. The second says, "You college boys come down here, drink too much, and cause us a lot of trouble. Well now, you are in trouble! We are taking you in for public drunkenness." They march us toward the intersection where they call a squad car to pick us up. Joey and I have not had anything to drink. It doesn't matter. Fred and Bill are so obviously drunk, and the police assume we've all had too much to drink.

I find out later the tiny town of Ocean Drive on the northern outskirts of Myrtle Beach funds its police department largely by arresting college students and releasing them after they post a substantial bail. All charges are dropped, and the police department has money to pay bills. It is a ninety-day (Memorial Day until Labor Day) cash bonanza for the police department.

In 1967, the police department hit a gold mine. College students that summer organize a massive gathering in Ocean Drive. A crowd estimated at 10,000 students descend on the tiny town. Two students play pool in one of the clubs the first night and get into a fight. Police enter the club and arrest them. The massive crowd outside will not let the police and the two students out the door. The police call for backup. With sirens blasting and blue lights flashing, police cars pull in from all directions. Students throw beer bottles at the police cars. Backup police from North Myrtle Beach arrive. Students are arrested by the dozen. Large refrigerated seafood trucks borrowed from a local shrimp company haul the students to jail. The jail cannot hold all of the estimated five-hundred students that are arrested. Police sit out buckets and trash cans. Students are told if they put all their money in the containers they can leave.[6]

So this night we stand on the street corner waiting for the squad car to take us to jail. Pastor Leroy prophesied that all the Howells are going to Hell. Well, I guess, I am taking the first step by going to jail.

I try to make my case to one of the officers that I have not had anything to drink. He looks at me with a "yeah right" look. Down the street comes another officer with two more intoxicated college students. It's going to be a profitable night for the department.

A silver Lincoln Town Car stops at the intersection. A window on the passenger side rolls down. It's an older couple. "We're lost," she says. "We're looking for the Ocean Drive Motel." I remember seeing it as we drove into town. The officers, slightly distracted by the approaching officer, can still hear me give directions to the lost woman.

The squad car pulls up to take us for at least one long night in jail and no telling what that will be like. The officers now have a dilemma: there are six intoxicated, or so they insist, college students but they can only transport four in the just arrived police car. The officer looks at me, studies me for a couple of seconds, and says harshly because he doesn't want to do this, "I heard you give those directions . . . maybe you are not drunk. You can go, and take your buddy (pointing at Joey) with you."

Fred and Bill head to the slammer, but Joey and I are "free birds." As we cross the street headed to the good times of The Pad nightclub, we watch the squad car with Bill and Fred speed away.

Indeed a fun place! College students from all over mingling and celebrating their youth and low impulse controls. Drinking, dancing, lots of conversation, but you have to shout above the music. Male and female hormones are in search of one another. Carloads of female students have arrived as well to match up with their male counterparts.

My first conversation, with a stunningly attractive woman who has made her way across the dance floor to talk to me, stays unforgettable. In front of me stands the woman of my dreams: shapely, tan, and eyes that sparkle. My first impulse says to me that this curvaceous, smiling, charming woman who wants to talk to me resides way out of my league. And she does. She is certainly three or four years older than me. She starts telling me stuff, "We go to the University of South Carolina. I'm a first-year graduate student in psychology. We like to come here every May before final exams and just have a good time before we have to go back and hit the books." Performance anxiety grips my vocal cords and my brain. I can't think of anything to say. So she says, "Is this your first time . . . here?" My entire body freezes with anxiety. Just enough air rests in my lungs to force past my vocal cords to say in a high pitched voice, "Yes ma'am." I know the instant those words leave my lips what I have done. Not a good start. She smiles, turns, and walks away.

As the evening goes on, things improve. I relax and have some good conversations. I am not looking to hook up with any young woman this evening. We must turn our attention to our problem. Our two friends are in jail. What do we do?

In talking to other guys in The Barrel, we learn from their experiences with the police and jail. All we need to do is come up with $150 each for their bail, and all will be forgiven. But we don't have $300 . . . maybe $30 between us. So we decide to find a telephone booth and call the fraternity house. It is Friday night and party night, and we are fortunate the phone is even answered. What we work out is that the fraternity president will get in touch with the fraternity faculty advisor and wire $300 via Western Union to their Myrtle Beach office.

With a plan in place, we return to the corner of Ocean Boulevard and our beach club familiarization tour. It is almost 4:00 AM when we finally hit our motel beds.

Around noon, we start to open our eyes. Dressed in cut-off jeans and brightly colored t-shirts, our sandaled feet hit the street in search of food. We are at the beach, but we do have some business to attend.

After a lunch of beach-burgers topped with shrimp and cocktail sauce, and hot golden brown onion rings drowned in cheese-sauce, we are off to find the Myrtle Beach Western Union office. We arrive at 1:45 PM. We both experience a wave of "oh no" disappointment, shame, and anxiety. The lettering on the door says "Saturday 9:00 AM until 1:00 PM." We can't get the money to free Freddie and Bill . We look at each other and silently communicate what we both know. We stayed out too late, slept too long, stuffed our stomachs, and let our friends down.

Not expecting our friends to be happy with us, we find the jailhouse and get permission to talk to our friends. Are they still our friends? They have not talked to anyone. Using their one allowed phone call, they ordered a pizza. We explain the situation and also break the news to them that the Western Union office is closed the following day (Sunday) and does not reopen until Monday at 9:00 AM. Disbelief and anger flush across their faces. "How could you sleep in and let us rot in this stinking jail?" We apologize profusely, but it does not help.

We learn Fred causes a stir in the jailhouse overnight. Fred has a rare genetic blood disorder, porphyria. Shocking to see for the first time, porphyria causes blue urine. In the bathroom with Fred, a jail policeman sees the blue urine. Accused of being on LSD, Fred has to explain about his genetic disorder.

More bad news, Joey kept a hawksbill knife (a pocket-sized knife but has a large curved blade like a hawk's bill) in his car glove compartment. On the trip down to the beach, Bill needed a way to open his bottled beer. When finished he put the knife in his pocket. The knife is perfectly legal in North Carolina, but in South Carolina, considered an illegal concealed weapon. Bill now needs another $150 for a total of $300 to get out of jail. When we come across a phone booth later, we call the fraternity house and put in an order for another $150 to be wired to Western Union.

We only plan to stay two nights, but the arrests cause us to stay an extra night. We do not have money for the room and food. We find a pawn shop (a thriving business from college students trying to raise bail money for their friends). All of our watches, radios, and jewelry are pawned to generate enough money for the room. Unfortunately, we have to pawn Bill and Fred's gear as well. Furthermore, we only brought enough clothes for two days. We start wearing Bill and Fred's clean clothes.

Monday morning, we rise in time to arrive at the Western Union only a few minutes after it opened. The clerk puts a stack of bills into an envelope and hands its to Joey, saying with a smile, "Got some friends in the slammer?" We shake our heads as we walk out the door.

At the police station, we hand the envelope to the releasing officer. Our two weary friends stumble out, looking like what theologian John Calvin (that I read later in life) called "total human depravity." They are still in the same clothes they wore on Friday while Joey and I are in their fresh clean clothes. We climb in the car, head back to college, and tell them we pawned all their valuables for our room rent. "Damn, what a trip!" Bill says, "A trip to the beach and I never saw the ocean or the sun, owe $300, and all my valuables are pawned." For a few moments, we all look at each other with some apprehension. Bill first, but then all of us, start roaring with laughter.

Sparking, Holy Liquor, Tuna

"Fools rush in where angels fear to tread."

ALEXANDER POPE

SUMMER COLLEGE BREAKS COME not as vacations for me. Fraternity brothers with wealthy parents hang around the country club pools all day and take long trips to the beach. I have to make money in the summer to live on while at college.

An hour's drive to Asheville, but a construction job there pays well. A friend and I leave at 6:00 AM in the morning to be at the job site by 7:00 AM. It is only a four-story building, but for a lad from Boonford, it is like a skyscraper. The guys who work year-round for the construction company resent the college boys. They give us the dirtiest, most difficult jobs. We accept our tasks though, just the pecking order.

Back in Boonford in the evening and after quick showers, we hang out with other college students who are working summer jobs at the mountain resorts like Eseeola Lodge and Little Switzerland Lodge. The students staff the restaurants that serve the summer tourists, and most of these places have small dormitories for their summer staff. These are pleasant memories of spending cool mountain evenings with new friends as we hang out in their dormitory rooms. Romance sometimes sparks, and sometimes it is just good conversation as we share stories from our various colleges.

As a college student, my mother occasionally asks me, "Are you sparking?" "Sparking" in mountain vocabulary is serious attraction between a young man and a young woman. "Flirting" usually precedes

114

"sparking." Lots of flirting usually happens before the sparking starts. When "flirting" is reciprocated, intense "sparking" starts.

"Sparking" (as brain science would later teach us) causes the dopamine levels in the brain to soar. Dopamine is the pleasure chemical in the brain. So the mountain folks were accurate in calling it "sparking." For the mountain folks, prolonged sparking leads into the next phase of a relationship called "courting" or "courtin." Courting is a monogamous (or at least it is supposed to be) period when the young man or young woman promises not to "flirt," "spark," or "court" with anyone else. The commitment was hard to keep because sometimes "sparks" fly between other young men and young women. If one "courts" another long enough in the mountains, one was expected to "get hitched."

Occasionally, a young couple's "sparking" fires up so intensely and the dopamine levels so euphoric, they "run off and get married." The legal marriage in North Carolina at the time was sixteen, but in South Carolina the legal age was fourteen. So in relationships where the young woman was not yet sixteen, they "ran off" to South Carolina to get hitched. The couple typically brings back a load of fireworks that could be legally purchased in South Carolina but not in North Carolina. When we hear a series of loud explosions lighting up the night sky in the community (and it isn't July 4th), we knew someone had "run off and got married" and had returned to celebrate. There were times when there were no celebrations. Sometimes parents are upset and angry that their daughter or son has "run off."

The legal age for marriage in South Carolina is now eighteen. However, a 1962 law allows a girl as young as twelve to marry if she is pregnant. *The Post and Courier* of Charleston, SC, estimated over 7000 young girls married older men legally under this law. In 1997, a sixty-year old man married a sixteen-year old girl.[7]

My father had a methodology for young men to select their wives. Crude criteria heard from his father and his father from his. I don't think he was kidding when he told a group of teenage boys: "Before you start courtin' a girl make sure she has good teeth and a good stomach." The incredible rationale was that a wife with bad teeth could cost the young man a fortune in dental work. "A woman with a good stomach," he explained, "is a woman who could eat anything." Times could get hard, and dietary choices might be limited.

One day it happened, unbelievably. I arrive home from college. Mark, a high school friend, wants to bring his new wife to meet me. Mark did not attend college. With a job in a local plant, he marries his high school "sweetheart." Becky is from another local town. I had never met her. My father, mother, and I sit on the porch as we watch Mark and Becky proceed up the driveway. They park their new brown 1970 Mustang. One of the lures of foregoing college and going to work in a local plant is having the money to buy a new car. Some young men found the temptation irresistible.

My father with his right-hand pours tobacco from a red Prince Albert can into a small paper held in his left hand. After rolling it up, he brings the little torpedo-like object up to his lips and licks one edge of the paper from end to end, sealing the tobacco inside. He then admires his work, puts the homemade cigarette into his mouth, and blows out a stream of gray smoke. He "studies" the newlyweds as they walk across the yard. My father called serious cognitive activity "studying." Often when I asked him permission to participate in some new activity or take a trip, he would say "let me study on it fer a while." He was not going to read a book or Google. He was going "to think about it."

Mark heard earlier my father's advice about picking a woman with "good teeth and a good stomach." My father makes a "quick study" that sunny day as the couple under inspection approaches us. Without even saying "hello" my father pronounces, "Mark, it looks like she has a good stomach on her." Fortunately, Becky is a good sport and familiar with this method of judging "human quality." She has not only a "good stomach" and "good teeth" but also is a believer in gender equality because she says with a intense smile on her face, "Well, what about Mark's stomach? Do you think he has a good one?" We are momentarily stunned by her quick wit, but then introductions are made. It was a teaching moment for Becky and a learning moment for us.

My father participated in some unusual customs and traditions. He had a most peculiar way of celebrating Christmas. The tradition was started by a neighbor, Roland Thomas. Roland was a survivor of World War II. He did not hit the beaches of Normandy but of Italy. With his company, he fought his way to Rome and Mussolini, the hated dictator of Italy and ally of Adolf Hitler. Roland Thomas was on the front lines as Rome fell into allied hands. In a battle north of Rome, Roland was shot in the face. The bullet, fortunately, came from the side and took off part of his chin, instead of penetrating his throat or brain.

Roland Thomas talked about how thankful he was to be alive and maybe that is why he started his unique Christmas Day ritual. A few minutes after seven in the morning on Christmas Day, Roland heads out the front door, gets into his Dodge Studebaker, and drives the short distance to our house. He stops in the driveway as close as he can get to the house. He blows his horn that my father has been expecting to hear. My father puts on his "cap and coat" (as he liked to call them) and goes out the door. He opens the door on the passenger side and slips into the seat, closing the door behind him. Roland reaches under the seat for his "Christmas liquor," as he calls it. It is a fifth of Wild Turkey, and he has another fifth under the seat in case it is needed. He peels back the brown bag, screws off the cap, and takes a big swig. Beaming with a smile, he offers the bottle to my father and proudly proclaims "Merry Christmas Jack!" My father takes a big gulp from the same bottle, smiles, and says, "Merry Christmas to you Roland!"

The Christmas festivities continue. With my father riding shotgun, Roland puts the car in reverse, turns around, and heads to the home of Sydney Burleson who has been eagerly awaiting the Christmas honk of the horn. Sydney gets in the backseat, takes a drink, and declares "Merry Christmas to all!." In a short time, the car has five passengers, men who have responded gladly to Roland Thomas's invitation and the communion liquor. In about an hour, the Christmas chariot of liquored up "wise men" are returned to their homes in time to watch excited children emerge from their bedrooms to see what Santa has brought them.

I work in a hosiery mill one summer. The same kind of hosiery mill that employed my mother her entire life but in a different town. It is monotonous, boring work, packing boxes of women's hosiery for shipment. The company based in New Hampshire established this plant in North Carolina because lots of inexpensive labor resides in the mountains. An extreme contrast exists as the New England accented executives walk through the plant talking to the local workers with their unique southern mountain accents. The locals toil away, making these northerners wealthy. The executives are charming and generate a devotion from these uneducated and paycheck desperate mountaineers.

Rodney and I work together packing boxes. He is in for life. Having dropped out of high school, he will have few if any future employment opportunities. The envy of many young men, he has the coolest car around, a 1966 baby blue Chevelle SS with 454 horsepower engine, dressed out in dual chrome exhausts and chrome mag wheels. Every evening, he drives around the little town of Spruce Pine, his left arm hanging out the window while the mighty Chevelle engine shakes the ground underneath.

Rodney could have played "The Fonz" (Arthur Herbert Fonzarelli), but Henry Winkler got the role in the sitcom *Happy Days*. Rodney has jet black hair styled just like The Fonz. Rodney has a couple of gold teeth that shine like precious jewels when he smiles.

The plant always closes a week for July 4. The plant also closes a week for Christmas, the only two weeks off for the employees. The New Hampshire executives have much more vacation time and additional perks. This Fourth of July vacation, my friend, Tuna, and I plan a trip to the beach. Unfortunately, the day before we are to leave for Ocean Drive, my car "broke down" and will not be ready until the end of the vacation week.

My sister helped me purchase an old sports car, a British-racing-green Triumph Spitfire. The purchase turns out to be a huge mistake. The wiring system was incredibly fragile. The previous owner apparently hooked up a battery charger incorrectly and fried the electrical system. Often, I drive the two-seater down the road with the top down, the happiest young man alive, and all at once the car just quits. A bump in the road causes a fragile wire to separate. Even worse, parts take weeks to arrive from England.

We decide to hitchhike to Ocean Drive beach. Tuna hitchhikes a lot because he doesn't have a car. Buddy Sheehan is Tuna's real name. Several years before, Buddy fishes in the South Toe River, largely polluted by mining companies who dump their mining residues into the river (no EPA to look after the environment then). Buddy comes up from the river and runs up the road shouting he has caught a tuna. Indeed, he has caught a fish from the murky polluted waters we have never seen before. The fish is huge!

At Uncle's grocery store, people gather to gander at Buddy's "tuna." Buddy insists he has caught a tuna. "It's a tuna, mama!" little Phil Burleson exclaims to his mother who has a bag of groceries on each hip. Old man Harry Wilson thinks otherwise, "It's not a tuna, but I don't know what it is." Rom Canipe pulls up in his beat-up pickup truck with ladders and tools stuffed into the bed of the truck and an oversized CB radio antenna on the roof of his truck. Rom is a well-thought of handy-man and noted trout fisherman. He studies the big fish a few minutes and declares, "Buddy, what you have there's a carp. It's not native to this river. It probably was in a pond on one of these farms around here. Somebody probably drained their pond and threw their fish into the river. Nice catch though. Must weigh twenty pounds or more."

Outside the store, Sheldon "Tis" Murphy sits. He spends most of his days on a bench. Uncle allows "Tis" to sit on the bench only after "Tis" promises to spit his tobacco juice into a big empty coffee can. Without Uncle's prohibition, "Tis" spits his Mammoth Cave tobacco juice on the concrete and makes an unsightly mess that Uncle insists will turn away customers. Mammoth Cave is a twist of chewing tobacco that is burn-your-mouth strong, and few men in the area are "man enough to chaw" according to Uncle.

Uncle made me clean up the wood shavings from Sheldon's whittling because his art attracted customers. Children begged their parents to take them to Uncle's store in hopes "Tis" might be completing a whittling project like a whistle or a toy gun. "Tis" often gave the completed project to a child. I saw children jump up and down with excitement to receive the wooden gift. If "Tis" did not have a sculpture, he always had a "piece of candy" in his pocket for the child. Children loved "Tis." If "Tis" had a large piece of basswood or balsa, he might sculpt a wooden chain or the "mysterious ball in the cage," a loose ball carved inside a small see-thru wooden box.

"Tis" gave a "mysterious ball in the cage" to a child from Atlanta. On their next trip to the mountains, the grateful parents brought "Tis" as a gift a diamond faced sharpening stone that was always in Sheldon's pocket. "Tis" carried the sharpest knife in the area. Women and men brought kitchen and pocket knives for "Tis" to sharpen, and in return, they would give him a dollar. I thought of "Tis" when as an adult I toured art museums in Europe and observed wooden altarpieces, like the Barnabas Altarpiece and Isenheim Altarpiece carved of basswood by sculptors like "Tis."

You could sit outside on that bench with "Tis" for days at a time and only hear him say two words "Tis" or "Not." He was as silent as God most of the time. When he spoke with his toothless smile, we took it to be as good as the word of God. A shopper like Lucille Conley might pull up to Uncle's store, park, and step out of the car. As she walks by in an effort to be friendly to "Tis" sitting on the bench, she says, "A pretty day, ain't it?" "Tis" wipes the tobacco juice away from the corners of his mouth with his shirt sleeve. "Tis" he states convincingly in his deep rattling, God-like, voice. That's all he would say, just "Tis." Sheldon convincingly shakes his head up and down when he utters "Tis." If he did not agree with something, "Not" thunders out of his mouth with a deep guttural rattle as he shakes his head from side to side.

"Tis" observes this great discussion about Buddy's monster fish. When Rom pronounces it a carp, "Tis" wipes the drooling tobacco juice away from both corners of his mouth which is a sign that he is about to speak. Everyone is silent and leaning forward as he declares "Tis." The deal is sealed. It's a carp, not a tuna. Unfortunately, Buddy creates himself a life-long problem.

Several older boys gather at the store. When everyone hears the pronouncement that the giant fish is a carp, one of the older boys, Elwood Spikes, says loud enough for everyone to hear, "Buddy, that fish ain't a tuna but you are! Your new name is Tuna!" Buddy shrugs it off and hoists his giant prize over his shoulder and heads home. Though things are going to be different from now on for Buddy.

When Buddy arrives at school on Monday morning and approaches his locker, someone has painted in big letters on his locker: TUNA! As he walks down the hall, his classmates say, "Hey Tuna!" Another student jeers, "Hey Tuna, you having a tuna sandwich for lunch?!" Kids can be unmercifully cruel to each other just to get a few laughs. Algebra teacher, Cory Cox who always smelled like cigarette smoke, makes the name Tuna indelible. Having heard the great tuna story already, Mr. Cox needs a student to come to the board to work on an algebraic equation. "I hear we have a student with a new name. Tuna would you come to the blackboard?" The students and Mr. Cox roar with laughter.

So Buddy is Tuna for as long as I knew him. He did try to exact some revenge and shake the name Tuna. Several days after the shaming in Mr. Cox's room and after Buddy begins to realize that he can't get rid of the name, he gets up one morning, goes to the kitchen, and grabs a bottle of fish oil from the cabinet. In the bathroom, he pours the fish oil into the palm of his hand and rubs it on the back of this neck. To make sure he has a creepy, strong fish odor, he puts more in his hand, pulls his shirt up, and rubs the oil over his chest.

The hysterical laughter begins soon after Buddy walks into the school because he smells like a dead fish that has been out in the hot sun for a couple of days. The entrance where his bus lets him off is on one end of the school building, and Buddy's homeroom is on the other end of the building. The fishy odiferous Buddy walks across the building and through the long hallway packed with students putting jackets and books in lockers. "He smells like a dead fish!" Linda Jones screams. Students put their hands over their mouths and noses, but they are laughing so hard they can't hold their hands up long.

Mr. Cox writes an equation on the blackboard as Buddy walks into the room. Hearing the students laughing behind him, Mr. Cox turns, and as he does, catches the first smell of Tuna. With his hand over his face, he steps forward, leans against his desk, and laughs until tears run down his glowing red cheeks. "I guess you're hoping we'll stop calling you Tuna if you come in here smelling like an old dead fish. Geez! You'll never live this down. You are now Tuna for life!" And yes he was.

Tuna and I stick out our thumbs early on a hot July morning. We are making a summer pilgrimage to the Mecca of beaches for college students, Ocean Drive. Everyone calls it OD. The beach is just north of Myrtle Beach, South Carolina. We have a full day of hitchhiking in front of us. Tuna is the Einstein of hitchhiking since he does not have a car. His mother never learned to drive, saying she was too "nervous." His father had his license revoked for driving under the influence on three occasions.

Out of necessity, Tuna studied different styles of "thumbing." He explains to me three different techniques. He demonstrates one style sticking the thumb up almost as high as possible over the head but about two feet to the side of the head. He states emphatically we will not use that style. "Startles people. Nobody will pick us up." He goes on "Lazy 'thumbers' let their arms hang down with their thumbing hand twelve inches off the knee. People don't like lazy people and figure they're just too lazy to work and buy a car."

We employ Tuna's scientifically proven method of placing the thumbing hand parallel to the hip and about sixteen inches off the body. He instructs me to smile, always difficult for me. The day before he told me to bring a tie. "Why do I need a tie? We're going to the beach?" I ask bewilderedly. "Just bring one!" Tuna commands. On the side of the road, we put on our ties, hold out our thumbs, and smile, like we won a girlfriend a teddy bear at the local carnival.

Several cars whiz by, but then we see the pleasing sight of a car's brakes lights. The car slows down and pulls over. Excited, we run to the car. "Where you fellers going with them ties on?" "Butane" Bennett asks. "We're going to the beach!" I say proudly. "With a damn tie on?" the man laughs out. "I can take you down the mountain to Marion, but that's as far as I am going," he says. "That would be great," Tuna says as he looks at me with a big smile that says I told you so.

Bobby "Butane" Bennett carries on his skin a sad story and bears a cruel nickname. As a teenager, he works on a car's muffler in a grease pit in a repair shop. Another employee flips a lit cigarette butt into the grease pit, and the grease ignites with a big "whoosh." By the time they pull Ross Bennett from the pit, he has second and third-degree burns over his entire body. His ears are now plastic, and his skin is horribly disfigured. Like everyone in the mountains, he gets a nickname that usually begins with the same letter as his last name.

The techniques of Tuna's "thumbing" get us to Marion, on to Charlotte, and then to Route 17, the much-traveled road from New York to Miami. When the Volkswagon Beetle opens its doors for us, we climb in. Two bonafide hippies share with us they are on their way from New York City to Miami. I am awed by the tie-dyed t-shirts, bell-bottom jeans, beads around the neck and wrist, and most of all the hair, nearly shoulder-length hair! I learn a new vocabulary: "Heavy, man" "Cool" "Far out." I'm sad when the VW lets us out at the intersection of Route 9 that goes into North Myrtle Beach and speeds on down Route 17.

"The country changing," I say to Tuna. "What with the war protests, the long hair, and grungy clothes. People our age want to be different."

Tuna looks at the sky, rolls his head around, and posits. "Yeah, I see it happening right now . . . the past is letting go and becoming the future."

"Tuna, I didn't know you were a durn philosopher!" I declare. We laugh.

A dirty, dented, ugly brown pickup truck, the bed loaded with watermelons, and a cab swirling with hazy tobacco smoke, volunteers to be our next ride. We put our bags on top of the watermelons as we slide into the front seat. "Where you boys going?" the man asks as he tokes on his pipe. We tell him the beach. He shakes his head like he already knew. The benevolent driver says we can have a watermelon when he lets us off. He explains he is a "watermelon wholesaler." He buys watermelons from local farmers and sells them by pickup load to large grocery stores along the coast of South Carolina. "It's a fine living in the summertime," he says, "but as the winter sets in I have to go further and further south to find watermelons. By Christmas, I'm done until the spring. Can't make no money going all the way to Florida for a load of melons."

When melon-man lets us off, we are not thinking about a free melon. A pounding rain slams the asphalt. Luckily, he lets us off at a small strip mall that has a telephone booth. Both of us cram into the booth to escape the downpour, and with the idea that we will call a taxi to take us the short distance to Ocean Drive. A big yellow phone book bound with a black cover hangs on a chain by the phone. Tuna looks in the yellow pages for a taxi company. Dropping a quarter in the slot on the phone, he spins the rotary button around several times until he has a ring on the other end. He talks briefly, hangs up the phone, and declares, "I've never called a taxi before, cause I've never ridden in a taxi before." Dawns on me I've never been in a taxi either.

We wait for the taxi. We wait for the taxi. And we wait for the taxi. Huddled together in the phone booth, almost an hour passes. "Tuna, are you sure you gave them the right location?" I ask. "I know I did. Look you can see the address on the front of that store, and I told them we would be in the phone booth." Tuna responds. Still, we wait.

Not many cars pull into the strip mall this abysmal, rainy evening. The few that do are shoppers. Finally, a car pulls up to the phone booth. Our luggage is sitting outside the entire time. I hope it is waterproof, but I doubt it. Grabbing our luggage we slide into the backseat of the taxi. "You boys picked a damn rainy night to be traveling. What's your destination?" The taxi driver asks. "Ocean Drive beach." I proudly declare. "That's not far." The driver says as he slips the transmission into drive and speeds away.

Fifteen minutes later we pull up in the heart of Ocean Drive. It is still raining but not a downpour. "That will be thirty dollars, boys." The driver says. "But that was only about ten minutes!" I protest. "Our company is in south Myrtle Beach, about forty miles from where I picked you up. We wondered why you called a taxi company in south Myrtle Beach when you were north of North Myrtle Beach. I have to charge you for my entire trip." The driver explains.

Tuna and I look at each other in disbelief. Tuna opens the car door, and hops out as he screams "Run!" In his haste, Tuna forgot his luggage, one bag, but easy for the taxi driver to grab as he looks at me firmly and says, "You ain't getting your luggage until you pay me my goddamn thirty dollars." A defeated Tuna crawls back into the car and says, "Okay, we'll see what we can do."

We pay the long-distance taxi driver. As he heads back south we scream at his tail-lights as if it might help. We are at the beach, but we have a new problem. We had not planned for a thirty-dollar taxi bill. Even if we find a cheap place to stay, we will have to cut our stay short.

We walk the streets, carrying our heavy water-soaked luggage, and hoping to find room in a cheap inn. Hungry tan and black cats are on top of a dumpster, trying to figure out a way to get in. Will that be us later on? A lot of the homes in the area are turned into boarding houses for beachgoers. Who wants to live in an area with college students and clubs bellowing out loud music and obscenities well into the night? The boarding houses are all too expensive for us. One boarding house clerk has some sympathy for these two weary, rain-soaked travelers. "I'm all booked up, or I would give you a really good deal since . . . you look like you've had a difficult journey. But if you go down to the next intersection, take a right, and the big ole white house on the right, probably has a room and a good deal."

Hopeful, we walk according to the clerk's directions. As we turn the corner, a skinny stray dog crosses in front of us. We find the big old white house and open the front door. A short, overweight, bald man, face as round as a full moon, sporting a dark four-day beard, and a dirty white t-shirt spotted with pasta sauce comes out from behind a curtain that covers an otherwise door-less doorway. "Young gentlemen, how in the hell are you?" the curmudgeon asks as he burps at the same time. "I just finished a late dinner. We had a frigging pipe break late this afternoon. Fucking water all over the place. I got the sum-a-bitch fixed though. Most of the folks here did not even know it happened. You know, they kind of slept through the damn whole thing. Hell, they sleep most of the time. God bless their hearts." Chilled in our wet clothes, we want to find out if he has a room.

"I do. I do. It ain't damn much. I don't got no air conditioning, and you'll have to share a bathroom with all the boarders on that floor, but it's a frigging bed, and looks like you gentlemen could use one."

"How much?" We ask. "Two dollars!" He snaps. "Now that's each!" He adds as he looks sternly at us,

Tuna and I glance at each other, and then back at him, "Okay, sure" as we pull out four damp dollar bills and hand them to the "inn-keeper."

"All frigging right then," beams the inn-keeper, "You are in room thirty-two on the third floor, but you be quiet as little angels as you go up, okay? We got some sum-a-bitches here who need their damn sleep."

As we go up the steps, Tuna whispers to me "that guy is the William Shakespeare of cussin." Tuna and I look at each other with big smiles on our faces. "Two dollars," Tuna whispers excitedly, "Heck we can stay a whole week."

After we exit the steps, the old knotty pine floors in the hall creak beneath our feet but that is not the loudest noise. Some of the bedroom doors are open. Loud moans and groans meet our ears as we walk toward room thirty-two. The sour stench of urine burns our nostrils.

"God, help me!" one elderly man tries to scream as we walk by, but it is a faint effort. He is old, real old. His hair is gray, and his skin is not only wrinkled but pale. His almost orange fingernails look like they have not been trimmed in months and his dark yellow toenails curl up under his toes.

In every room where the door is not shut, we see suffering and agony with labored breathing and in the best cases loud snoring. I whisper to Tuna, "I think they're all dying." Tuna makes a sad and apprehensive face. "It's a death house!" We've rented a room in a poor man's hospice that doesn't have a medical staff, just a place to die.

Room 32, stark and barren, greets us. A metal clothes rack rests against one wall with an assortment of worn black, metal hangers. Dirty smeared walls, probably not painted in several decades, greet us. Against another wall is a small wooden chest with drawers that either won't pull out or fall out. The brass bed is impressive, probably left by wealthy own-ers before the college kids took over the town. "There's enough dirt on this floor to plant potatoes." Tuna cracks.

Taking off shoes, socks, pants, and shirts, all still wet, we turn back the bedspread and both of us gasp. The sheets are lemon-like in color and stiff like thin cardboard. I fully expect them to break into pieces. They don't, and we slide between those sheet relics that might have been left by previous owners as well.

Voices and cursing wake us a few minutes after midnight. Four Ma-rines on leave from Fort Bragg, North Carolina, checked in because this place has the only vacancy on this holiday weekend. They are unhappy with their rooms. I hear one marine exclaim. "This place is a frigging dump. There are old men dying in every room!" Another Marine with a deep booming voice says, "Let's get out of this hell hole. I'll drive back to Bragg before I stay here." A third voice says, "Yeah, our barracks are better than this." Tuna and I don't know whether to laugh or cry.

The next morning brings bright sunshine and glistening white beaches. For evening entertainment, we stick out our thumbs again and catch a ride south to the original Myrtle Beach and the Pavilion Amuse-ment Park at 9th Avenue North and Ocean Boulevard, eleven acres of rides and thrills. The Pavilion is the original center of attraction for Myrtle Beach. It is a circus and a carnival all rolled into one, and a brilliant mar-keting ploy by the original developers of the jewel of the Grand Strand. Delightful screams ring out from anxiety-seeking roller coaster riders. Ferris wheels turn adorned with every color of light and highly pleased vacationers, many on that long-anticipated week off for the Fourth.

We step off the Hurricane, a prized coaster ride with its two hundred-foot drop and hair-pin turns. We see a guy with jet black hair jelled to his head and a pack of cigarettes in his rolled up shirt sleeve. He turns, smiles. We see his glistening gold teeth, one on each side of his mouth. It's Rodney and a friend from the plant back home! We tell him about the boarding house from hell and explain to him we are cutting our stay and thumbing home the next day.

"Just ride with me and Tim. We have to go back tomorrow. My baby sister is getting hitched to some jerk on Saturday, and I gotta go. Just meet us here at the "Pav-ah-lon" at noon tomorrow. We're going to take some more rides on the Hurricane late morning and then head home." I suppose it was the lack of education because pronunciation was not a strong point for Rodney. Pavilion to him was "Pav-ah-lon," but it communicated.

We wake up the next morning thoroughly excited. We have a ride home, no thumbing in torrential downpours. Plus, we ride in one of the coolest cars "known to man," Rodney's 1966 baby blue Chevelle with 454 'horses' and chrome glistening like diamonds. We go through the main streets of more than two dozen little towns on the way home, and arms are hanging out of four windows. We could not be prouder if we were in a Macy's parade on Thanksgiving Day.

Blue Baptism and Antenna of Antennas

"And now what are you waiting for? Get up,
be baptized and wash your sins away, calling on his name."

ACTS 22:16

EVERYBODY TALKS ABOUT A big development in Boonford, a shocking event at Born Again Church's farm pond turned baptismal pool. Chester Connelly, like so many middle-aged men in the area, struggled through school and could not have been happier when he dropped out at sixteen. He got a swing-shift job at a local plant. He works "days" for two weeks and then the "graveyard shift" for two weeks. The 11:00 PM to 7:00 AM shift is called the graveyard shift because the person can never adjust to the disturbances to the natural sleep rhythms. Anyone who ever worked that shift for long knows it is not healthy. In recent years medical studies confirm their learned experiences.

Chester stands on the banks in his white baptismal robe with his beautiful family, wife Flossy and three girls. Their families kept the Scotch-Irish DNA pure, only marrying their own kind. They are all fair-skinned, sparkling blue eyes, and glowing blonde hair with a touch of red pigment. They certainly look like they descended from Picts and Gaels (later to be called Scots) that had intermarried with invading fierce Norsemen centuries ago in their native lands that today we call Scotland. By the end of the ninth century, Vikings indeed settled in some Scottish areas.

A striking attractive family anxiously waits on the bank, their blond locks shining brightly in the mid-day sun in a cloudless sky. They are surrounded by the church members from Born Again Church, just chastised and brow-beaten by Reverend Leroy before they enjoyed dinner (called lunch in most places) on the church grounds.

Flossy and the children, already baptized, attend church for two years, but Chester held out until his mother died. Pastor Leroy "preached her funeral," and Chester swore to be forever grateful and joined the church. His mother's death and his grief facilitated a change in Chester. Until her death, he had never cried. He thought crying was a sign of weakness and any show of emotion was for sissies. But Chester felt different now and "gave his life to the Lord." As all the church members did, he gave his life to Pastor Leroy as well.

After some introductory remarks about "the irresistible call to salvation from our Lord Jesus Christ" and how the "hounds of Heaven" are in constant pursuit of every unrepentant sinner, a short scripture reading, and a long eloquent prayer (including condemnations on just about everything "secular"), Pastor Leroy invites Chester into the "waters of baptism unto eternal life."

Chester comes from a family of large-boned and wide framed people, ancestors perhaps bred for war by ancient warring Vikings. Questions go through the minds of several church members on the bank, "How will Pastor Leroy lower this massive man into the water? And hold him there as he likes to do?"

Pastor Leroy looms as no small man either. Not as tall as Chester, he is thick with large muscular arms. Pastor Leroy's ancestors probably came from eastern Europe, perhaps Slavic, maybe mixed with some lower European DNA. His dark, thick hair is a perfect contrast to Chester's fair features.

Confidently, Pastor Leroy asks Chester if he repents of his sins and is ready to be reborn in the waters of baptism to eternal life. Just as confidently, Chester proudly proclaims, "I repent of all my sins. I am ready to be born again!" Chester's daughters look away feeling a little embarrassed by the drama and look around to see if any of their friends are in attendance. Chester's wife, Flossy, beams out a smile full of pride. She prayed every night for years for this wonderful day.

Chester goes into the water guided by the controlling arms of Pastor Leroy. First, his buttocks hit the water, then his back and shoulders as Pastor Leroy says, "This is your last glimpse of a man of this world, a sinner. He will come out of these baptismal waters reborn in the image of Christ!" Finally, Chester's head goes beneath the water. For a few seconds, his golden locks float near the surface.

"My fellow Christians," Leroy declares as he holds Chester under the dark waters, "If anyone here also wants to be born again, start to come forward. We have a white gown of salvation for you. You just have to repent of your sins and give your life to Jesus Christ, the author of our salvation. Come to salvation's shores!"

Careful eyes observe that Pastor Leroy is beginning to strain from the weight of big Chester Connelly. Pastor Leroy begins to lift Chester out of the waters of salvation. Shrieks explode from the people on the banks. "Oh my God, he's blue!" screams Flossy Connelly. Chester's children burst into loud crying. Women cover their mouths before they too are overcome with emotion. Several of the men leave the bank and wade toward Pastor Leroy, who for once in his adult life is speechless and without an immediate explanation.

The Pastor momentarily releases Chester who goes back under the water, but the men from the bank are there to grab arms and legs and take Chester to the shore. Flossy goes to her husband. A neighbor escorts the girls toward the parking lot. Chester is not breathing. He is a bruised-looking blue. He suffers a deadly heart attack at a moment never to be forgotten. The lack of oxygen and cool water temperatures turn his skin a purplish-blue. A frightening sight everyone sees.

Pastor Leroy steps on the shore a few feet from the blue body of Chester Connelly. The church people in attendance don't know what to do. Most want to leave, but Pastor Leroy has not dismissed them.

"Let's pray!" blasts the powerful voice of Pastor Leroy. All dutifully bow their heads even as tears roll down cheeks and sensations of fear and anxiety sweep through their bodies.

"Oh Lord, you have chosen to take this man, our brother in Christ, Chester Connelly, and we do not know why. We do not understand your wisdom or your ways. He leaves behind a loving and lovely family. Maybe he was not ready for your grace and salvation, we do not know. Maybe his sins were too great to be forgiven at this time of his baptism, we do not know. Maybe you just need him in the employment of Heaven. We will miss him and grieve him. In the name of the giver of life, Christ the Lord. Amen." All the people said, "Amen" except Chester's family.

Bill and Jewell Forbes drive home from the baptism when Jewell asks Bill, "Did you hear what Pastor Leroy said about Chester not being ready for salvation and maybe his sins were too great?" Bill responds, "Yep, I heard that, and he said it right there where Flossy and the children could hear it."

The "Blue Baptism" and Pastor Leroy's interpretation of Chester's death in the salvific waters of baptism as judgment from God becomes the first slippage in the esteemed and elevated stance of Pastor Leroy in the church and the community. Many of the church members live in fear of the judgment and power of Pastor Leroy. A few conversations behind closed doors begin to question his authoritarian rule over the congregation and his theological shaming of a dead man, Chester Connelly.

My mother tells me about the Blue Baptism as soon as I get back from the beach. "Lordy, David, Chester's funeral was awful. Pastor Leroy said in the funeral that Chester was taken by the Lord because he submitted to baptism with an unclean heart. Flossy stood up when he said that and pointing her finger at the Pastor said, 'You killed Chester. You held him under the water too long! It was you! You killed a good man!' Flossy's and Chester's families all stood up and walked out as Chester's brothers took the casket, put it in a pickup truck, and buried him in a cemetery in another community. David, I don't know what is going to happen in this community. Everybody's upset. Some siding with Flossy, and others with the Pastor. I never liked the man, myself."

After gall bladder surgery, my father rests in the hospital. We gather in the waiting room at the tiny hospital. The waiting room is shared by families with relatives in ICU, surgery, or general hospital. In a hospital room next to the waiting room is a man, I never got his name, who was recently diagnosed with esophageal cancer. Terrified about his fate, he loudly warns everyone within the sound of his voice the perils of not giving their lives to Jesus. Apparently, the nurses heard these dire warnings and calls to salvation for several days, so they mostly ignore him. A visitor hearing these loud, booming, calls for repentance and salvation for the first time is spooked. I was, for it is unexpected and scary loud. Sitting in the waiting room, I notice a large man with jet black hair and bushy eyebrows coming down the hall. Pastor Leroy! He either does not see the damned Howell clan in the waiting room or simply ignores us. He is there to visit the cancer patient turned evangelist. In a few moments, they are praying loudly together. Relieved, we see the Pastor's backside walking down the hall and away for us.

In a few weeks, I'm back at college for my final year. I develop a relationship with a stunningly attractive young woman attending a private college in Raleigh. Her eyes are sparkling blue, hair the color of sweet yellow honey, and smells like fresh flowers. My parents are out of money sending three kids through college. "Jack and Lena are 'broke' puttin those three young'uns through college," say the locals. I sell my car to pay tuition for that final year. I am smitten, in love head over heels, with this young woman. From a wealthy family, her annual college tuition is more than my parents' annual incomes combined. She sports around in her own new yellow Volkswagen Beetle with a black convertible top and often visits me on weekends.

Our relationship becomes more and more serious. She doesn't know how poor I am, but she will find out eventually. I invite her to meet my parents. She can decide if our societal and economic gaps are too much for her. I devise a plan that turns out to be similar to the "exposure therapy" I later learn in training to be a psychotherapist. Exposure therapy assists clients in reducing anxiety. If there is a fear of flying, for example, the person will spend some time in a flight simulator, maybe some time sitting in a small plane (without a take-off), and then some time on top a tall building, etc. Gradual exposure in small doses to the anxiety-causing trigger.

With the top down and her stunningly gorgeous hair blowing in the wind, she drives as we pass through Asheville and wind our way along the mountain road toward Burnsville and eventually Boonford. In the little community of Swiss, a house is badly in need of repair. Abandoned old cars and bashed-up pickup trucks rest in the front yard. Chickens roam the yard. Pigs grunt in a pen in the back yard. I ask her to turn into the driveway. Glancing at her eyes, they are about to pop out of her head.

"Honey, it ain't much but it's home." I humbly suggest.

She takes a deep swallow.

"Oh, this ain't it. I'm just kidding. We have another thirty miles to go." I say before she has a chance to speak. She takes a deep relaxing breath. When we arrive at the modest little rancher my father built with his own hands in his spare time, it didn't seem nearly as bad.

The monster television antenna my father built behind our house interests her. He constructed this in the early days of television after seeing the blueprint in a *Popular Mechanics* magazine at work. The scrap pile at the mine provides all the materials he needs: four large metal poles, large roll of wire, and insulators. The four poles are set about fifty feet apart forming a perfect parallelogram. He strings wire through the insulators from pole to pole. Finally, a wire stretches to the house and attaches to the big television with a rear tube that looks like a cement mixer. We already have an outside antenna, a classic, store bought model, like everyone in the community. The little community of Boonford nestled between several towering mountains only receives one channel, no matter how expensive the store bought antenna is. WCYB serves Bristol, Kingsport, and Johnson City, Tennessee. Every household wants to receive a North Carolina channel (Asheville, Charlotte, Raleigh), but the tall mountains block the signals for most.

My father works on the antenna of antennas for a couple of weeks in his spare time: digging the holes, putting the poles into concrete, waiting for it to harden, and stringing the wire. The construction creates a good deal of excitement in the community. A rumor is Jack Howell will be able to get every station in the southeastern United States. Pappy Price jokes the Russians might see it from outer space and bomb us. My father invites several of his friends over on a Saturday morning for the first viewing of this new-age technology. The friends invite other people. Families start arriving at 9:00 AM. Cars park on both sides of the road leading to our house. As many people as can crowd into our small living room. The final wire is attached. The television is turned on. The antenna works! But we still only get one channel! Some initial disappointment sweeps over us, but then everybody gets a laugh at the monster antenna that brings us the same channel.

On Fridays, I often hitchhike the four hours from western North Carolina to Raleigh to see her. Since my classes resume Monday, I need to return to my college by Sunday evening. One Sunday afternoon, I get a late start for my hitchhiking back across the state. My last ride puts me out on the outskirts of Hickory at 10:30 PM, still about two hours from campus. I stand on the side of the road and wait for cars. Thirty minutes pass, five cars go by, but none stop. I might be forced to spend the night on the side of the road. I figure my duffle bag makes a good pillow. What would I do for a blanket? Increasing chilling air penetrates my clothes.

A car comes up the road at a high rate of speed. The car streaks by me. Tires squeal as brakes are applied. The car fish-tails slightly, but the driver does not lose control. Surprised, I see the car backing up, which is not a problem because no other traffic comes up the road. Red tail-lights come toward me. I see blue like the ocean. A blue corvette stops beside me. The passenger window rolls down. An old friend from high school, Mike, who also goes to the same college, says in a parental disapproving tone, "David, what are you doing out here on the side of the road in the middle of the night?" I quickly explain.

Three people already crowd inside this two-seater Corvette. Mike and his friend, who owns the Corvette, are returning from Ocean Drive Beach. At the beach, Mike meets a young woman, who attends our college and who is now sitting in his lap. He talked her into riding back with him. They try to figure out where to fit me. I eventually crawl into the small space behind the two seats with all the duffel bags and coolers on top of me.

Even After Breaking Jesus' Crayons?

"Forgiveness is the final form of love . . ."
REINHOLD NIEBUHR

GRADUATE SCHOOL AT THE end of the final academic year appears financially impossible. We struggle to pay the tuition and expenses for four years, and I didn't want to burden my parents working at minimum wage anymore. The best thing, I figure, is to get a job. A position is available with a small company in Southside Virginia. The first thing I notice about Southside Virginia is the blatant racism.

In full disclosure, I joined a fraternity in college that claimed Robert E. Lee as its "spiritual founder" and "moral role model." The president and vice president of the local fraternity dressed in white robes and hoods for the annual meeting. The president in this meeting was to be addressed as "Most Worshipable Grand Master." The fraternity brothers and I never thought about the racial implications and KKK-like history of the organization. We simply liked this group of guys and wanted to be part of this social club on campus. It might be that the white residents of Southside Virginia would want to claim the same naiveté.

An incident on campus in my senior year brings the issue into focus. I finish my work hours managing the billiards room at the University Student Center. Since a big exam is the next day, I bring my book bag with me and walk up the stairs to the conference room where I could study for a few hours before going back to the noisy fraternity house. Often the case, I wear my bright red fraternity parka with the fraternity initials in gold letters on the front. I study for a few minutes when a group of African-American students enter the room. They reserved the conference room for a meeting of the executive committee of the Black Student Union, and a member of an exclusive white fraternity is in the room. They expressed displeasure with what the fraternity stood for historically. I did not know I was racially insensitive. My parents taught me all people are created equal, and I was to respect all people regardless of the color of skin. So, I am shocked that I am seen this way, but the experience did help me become more aware.

The racism in Southside Virginia shocks me. The small company has "virtual" slaves, a kind of feudal system. These are African-American families living on company land in small shacks without indoor plumbing. Each generation of men goes to work for the company, dropping out of school, when strong enough to do the manual labor. It is a never-ending cycle of poverty. I ask the company president, "Why don't you put bathrooms in these houses where your employees live?" He glares at me and snaps, "Their kind, they would just tear it all to pieces. You can't help them. They stumbled over diamonds over there in Africa for thousands of years."

These people live in fear of the company president. They have no options. Without significant education, they have no employment options. Most are large families and are dependent for survival upon the minimum wages paid to them. One day the president said, "If the negro ever loses his fear of the white man, we will have a problem."

Although displaying no signs forbidding entrance to non-whites, local restaurants serve whites only. Everyone knows it. Public schools are integrated, but most white children attend private academies. Like most America, Sunday morning services are segregated as the white folks gathered to proclaim how much they love Jesus. Even among the whites, a layered society exists. Wealthy whites owning businesses and large farms call their white workers "common." Older white males insist on being addressed as "Mr." A scorning look is cast if they are called by their first names. The wealthy whites insist that all others show "proper manners." Women are addressed as "Yes, Ma'am" or "No, Ma'am."

With the party days of college behind me, life turns much more serious. "Making a living" is central. A new awareness settles in me. Many friends die along the way. Two more friends from high school die shortly after I graduate from college. Both die from melanoma with their ancestors coming from England and Wales like me. The sun's rays are not kind to those of us whose ancestors are from northern Europe. I worry about cancer and other terminal illnesses. My hair starts to fall out (due to male pattern baldness). My father dies. Did he go to Hell? The curse was put on all the Howells by Pastor Leroy. My father did not go to church. With a social anxiety disorder, my father found it too painful to attend church, but did he condemn his own mortal soul? Or was he always destined for Hell? I experience the throes of an existential crisis.

I find calming relief when I join a church. In a segregated congregation in Southside Virginia, I profess my faith and receive Christian baptism. Delmar O'Donnell in *Oh Brother Where Art Thou?* was no more elated when he was baptized: "Well that's it, boys. I've been redeemed. The preacher's done warshed away all my sins and transgressions. It's the straight and narrow from here on out, and heaven everlasting's my reward."[8]

Soon, I teach Sunday School and lead a mid-week Bible class. Two local young pastors just out of seminary make an incredible impression on me. My work is boring, meaningless work (at least it seems to me) while they are involved in work that matters, helping people better their lives through spiritual growth and community action. I want to make a difference and my life to have a purpose. Several times per week after work, I travel with an evangelist and "give my testimony" at church revival meetings. Deeply intrigued by Jesus of Nazareth, my ambition is to know his teachings intimately.

Looking back, I think my narcissistic streak gets inflamed about this time. I start imaging myself as a persuasive preacher, helping people see the eternal, and find purpose for their lives. On the slippery slope to seminary, I am fascinated with preaching! Obsessed, I read sermons by Barbara Lundblad, James Forbes, Barbara Brown Taylor, Edmund Steimle, Tom Long, and others. From one perspective, it must have seemed odd this person, whose last two appearances at church were as a devil's minion on a crayon breaking and cupcake ruining rampage and as a voyeur to see the "crying preacher," is now captivated with preaching.

My Christian formation rapidly accelerates. I have much reason to distrust and resent authority and authority figures. They condemned me to Hell, and even a Boy Scout troop leader, supposed to be "trustworthy" and "honorable," tried to poison me. I saw rampant and disgusting racism in the Christian church. Later in therapy, my therapist shares an interesting insight with me. He was from the Catholic tradition, and so he used that language. He said he saw a lot of priests who had absent fathers and who in turn wanted to be the "good father" they never had. I certainly had an absent father, so it seemed to fit. Later in training to be a therapist, I learn this is one of the more "sophisticated" defense mechanism of the unconscious. "Sublimation of Needs" unconsciously drives behavior and even career decisions. The doctor might have a deep fear of dying and always wants a doctor with him or her. A trial attorney might have unresolved family issues and unconsciously want to argue his or her case against the sibling (opposing attorney) and to the father or mother (judge). A person with anger and aggressive issues might decide to make a "killing" on Wall Street. Was my unconscious motivation to ministry an effort to liberate others and me from the threats and fear of Hell? Consciously at least, my desire was to become a persuasive preacher guiding people to my understanding of the truth, which at the time was an evangelical understanding of the truth. In the years ahead, my pastoral identity evolves and changes.

My evangelical fervor causes me to apply to Gordon Conwell Seminary in Boston where I am accepted. A family situation makes it impractical to attend. I apply to Union Theological Seminary in Richmond, VA. My application denied because I am not grounded well enough in the necessary academia to be successful. On the fast track to seminary, my church background is very limited. Determined, I apply to Southeastern Baptist Theological Seminary in Wake Forest, NC. The seminary since was "taken over" by the extremely conservative side of the Southern Baptist denomination. At the time, the seminary has a high-quality layer of professors who look at the Christian tradition and biblical studies through the eyes of the best scholarship. A Harvard PhD graduate, for instance, is installed as a theology professor. We study classical theology, liberation theology, process theology, and much more.

Terrified, I start classes. I have a business degree and not a religious studies background. I have studied the Bible from cover to cover, read some of the writings of C.S. Lewis, but not much more. A New Testament professor calls me into his office after the first day of class and explains he knows my background (through a mutual friend). In his office, the professor looks over his glasses at me. I will never forget his words, "People with a background like yours have a really hard time here, and most don't make it." Maybe he said more, and maybe something encouraging and affirming, but that is all I remember. Doubly terrified, I resolve to give seminary my best 'boy from the mountains' shot. I study hard.

In seminary, students must master the original languages of the Bible: Hebrew of the Old Testament and Greek of the New Testament. (Theologically, I now prefer First Testament and Second Testament but that is a story for another time.) I had a small exposure to Greek in elementary school. Our fifth-grade teacher with a furious temper is feared and avoided. If provoked to anger, his voice rises to a screech and while shaking his raised index finger at the class declares: "I don't want to hear one 'iota' of noise out of this class. Not one 'iota'!" What was this "iota" we wonder? Frankie Laws says his mother looked it up in a dictionary at home and shared with us that an "iota" is an accent mark in the Greek language. So at least I knew that when I start my seminary Greek class.

I study, and Greek grammar comes easy. My grammar exams are perfect, and my translations are flawless. The professor approaches me and suggests I might want to pursue a PhD in Greek and teach. Flattered, I knew the jury was still out. The first semester focused on learning grammar and translation. In the second semester, we read Greek aloud in class. I've always had trouble remembering pronunciations of words that I rarely use (like Rodney back in the plant). Perhaps my brain doesn't want to waste memory space on seldom-used words. When it is my turn to read aloud, I butcher the readings. It is embarrassing. The professor never again suggests an advanced degree in Greek.

As part of a homework assignment, I translate Greek one afternoon and discover that the Greek word typically translated as "born again" should more accurately be translated "born from above." After checking with the professor to see if this is accurate, I chuckled to myself and wondered if I should go back to Boonford and tell them they need to change the name of their church from Born Again Church to Born From Above Church. I decided that should not be my first evangelistic crusade.

In Hebrew class the next year, my mountain accent collides with Hebrew. The first time the professor asks me to read in class he stops me and says, "David, you read Hebrew with a decidedly southern accent." Familiar with the geography of Israel, I said, "Down about Jericho." The professor shook his head, "Oh no, David, down about Eilat." Eilat is on the Red Sea in extreme "southern" Israel.

On the other hand, my background came in handy for my job during seminary. I worked the three to eleven shift in a factory making street-sweepers. Mostly, I operated a drill press, drilling holes in large pieces of metal. During the day, I dialogued with professors about process theology and the historical-critical method, but during the evening, I was just one of the guys trying to "make a living."

With study, I post excellent grades the first two years in seminary. I apply and transfer to Union Theological Seminary that had previously denied my entrance. The church I joined was Presbyterian. I thought it best to graduate from a Presbyterian seminary. Union did not accept all of my transfer credits so I spent one and one-half years there.

Union Theological Seminary experiments with a new curriculum design. September is one course. October through early December is the standard design of four or more classes. The second semester follows the same format.

"The Theology of Reinhold Niebuhr" starts my coursework. Niebuhr was an American theologian whose seminal works were *The Nature and Destiny of Man* (this was before inclusive language) and *The Children of Light and The Children of Darkness* describing a kind of Christian realism that Niebuhr took to politics and public affairs. During his presidency, I heard Barack Obama refer to Niebuhr and the realism needed in pubic policy.

The entire grade for the September course consists of a final multi-part essay exam, and the grade is simply "Pass or Fail." I think I have a good handle on the material and expect a pass grade. Grades are to be posted on the professor's door by a certain date. On the date, I confidently go to verify my Pass. I cannot believe my eyes when I scroll down the alphabetized list and beside my name is Fail. I immediately knock on the professor's door. Invited in, I explain I know the material, and this must be a mistake. He promises to re-read my essays. He is up against a book deadline and says it might be several weeks.

The failing grade disorients me. This is the seminary that originally refused my entrance. Now I failed the first course! Are their academic standards that much higher than the Baptist seminary? Furthermore, my father said I would not make it at college. Maybe, he meant seminary? And Pastor Leroy's curse always looms. The next round of October to December courses begin. I am worried, depressed, and to make matters worse I developed a deep sinus infection that lasts until the end of the year. Antibiotics do not help. I feel bad, low energy, and depressed.

Every time I visit the professor's office starting in late October, he waves me off. In his scratchy voice, he says, "Come back in a couple of weeks" and motions me out the door. In late November, I knock on the door. Finally, he invites me into his office. He starts apologizing profusely, "I don't know what happened. I must have started reading your essay, put it down, picked up another one, but put the grade on yours. You actually did a nice job."

Courses at Union challenge us. The professors like to say, "We want it to be at least as difficult as law school." With new winds in my sails,

I finish all my coursework in good shape. About to graduate I need a church. I fill out a "professional information form" with the local denominational office, have several interviews with church "search committees," preach a few "trial sermons." I receive a couple of job offers ("a call" in the church). Because of family considerations, I accept "a call" to a Southside Virginia church in a small town. Having lived in Southside Virginia, I knew what it was like but hoped the church would be different.

Before I leave the seminary, I pay a visit to my homiletics professor. With only a few sermons in my files, I ask him for a recommendation: "Is there a preaching journal he would recommend that would help me with my sermon preparation?" Immediately he answers, "There's isn't one. They're all just collections of cheap illustrations and not built on solid biblical scholarship. Don't waste your money!" Surprised, I filed that feedback away in my mind: Not one solid preaching journal!

Within the first week at the church, I experience a baptism by fire. An infant dies. I use all my training and pastoral skills to comfort the family but that was an impossible task at that point. During the service, the mother leaves her seat, runs to the front of the church, and throws herself on the casket, wailing at the top of her voice. Some women of the church try to comfort her and get her to release her tight grip on the tiny casket. She would not. Finally, the husband persuades her to let go. I bring the service to a close for the mother is decompensating quickly in deep grief. The cemetery and grave are beside the church. The father hoists the casket on his shoulder and tells the congregation, "Follow me." He leads us through the church door and into the cemetery where I preside over the committal. "Oh my," I think. "This is a tough line of work."

The grandparents invite all those at the church to their home after the service for a communal meal. In the south when someone dies, friends and family cook and bring enormous portions of food to the grieving family. So it makes sense to invite everyone to help eat the delicious and plentiful renderings of several different types of fried golden chicken, oven-baked breaded chicken, potato salad, deviled eggs, fresh home-made biscuits, creamed corn, slaw, and an assortment of cakes and pies.

At the feast of bereavement, I enjoy a conversation with the grandfathers, both farmers. They are not men who express deep feelings, but they do talk about the child's sudden death. One grandfather, shaking his head, says, as he gnaws on a chicken leg, "It's a terrible thing what has happened." The other grandfather, downing a deviled egg, reflects for a moment. Then he says honestly and openly, "These things happen." In

seminary, I studied a lot of theology, pastoral theology, and the philosophical Problem of Evil (If God is good and all-powerful, why is there
so much evil and suffering in the world?). At that moment for those two
men grabbling for some kind of meaning and hope from this tragedy,
"these things happen" is a comfort to them. For thirty-five years, "these
things happen" might be the best theological explanation I hear for The
Problem of Evil (also called Theodicy). Suffering and death are parts of
the natural order, of creation, and not divine determinism or Godly punishment or divine negligence.

My pastoral baptism of fire continues. Within the first year, another
tragedy strikes. Janice is a lovely and sweet senior in high school. Unfortunately, her boyfriend is not. She breaks up with him. I learn later
he probably could be diagnosed with Borderline Personality Disorder.
People with Borderline Personality Disorders cannot tolerate rejection.
Fearing abandonment, they experience intense emotions and act impulsively. Janice lives on a farm. The father rises at 4:00 AM and heads to
the barn to milk the cows. The boyfriend knows the father's schedule.
Waiting outside the farmhouse, the boyfriend slips through the unlocked
kitchen door after the father is out of sight. The boyfriend carries a double
barrel shotgun with one cartridge for Janice and another for himself. A
gruesome scene unfolds. The community and church are shocked. I visit
the family and officiate at the funeral. It is a terrible time. Such a lovely
human being taken for no good reason. It seems I cannot get away from
death, but that is the profession I chose.

Overall, my preaching suffices, I hope. The response, although not
bad, is a little sobering. After writing my weekly sermon, I often rehearse
in the empty sanctuary. The great preachers in the big city churches probably don't have to practice at all, just comes naturally to them. I later learn
a preacher from Georgia who became a civil rights activist rehearsed his
sermons about the only way he could. John Lewis goes outside his modest house and preaches to the chickens. Maybe I would have been a better
preacher had I some chickens.

Nevertheless, my fascination with preaching remains: How is it that
spoken words can help people change their lives? One of the most incredible experiences is to struggle with a sermon all week, and then struggle
with the delivery, with thoughts like "I should have chosen another
career." Then, during a farewell greeting at the church door or maybe
during a phone call during the week, someone says "That sermon meant

so much to me!" or "That's just what I needed!" Internally, I scratch my theological head . . ."how did that happen?"

Low moments happen in ministry. Some Sunday mornings pastors don't feel like they have anything much significant to say, but they have to go through the motions. The Reverend Gardner Taylor, pastor of the highly successful 14,000 member Concord Church in New York City and called the "Dean of American Preachers" and the "poet laureate of American Protestantism," shared that on some Sunday mornings when driving to his church he would observe laborers working on building projects and wish he could trade places with one of them. He said sometimes he didn't feel up to the responsibility of preaching.

I begin my ministry aggressively, too aggressively. A capable pastor, I add new members to the church. Most of the new members are college-educated, professionals, and progressive, but an old south uneducated group lurks in the church hoping to someday sink their teeth into a "liberal." Once I led a Bible study and divided the group into small groups for discussion. Several church members went to the church governing board with accusations that I led séances. But it isn't the small groups that infuriate them. I organize an Interfaith Council for the town and surrounding community. For the first time, white and black churches plan joint Christmas and Easter services but only at a neutral site, like a school gymnasium. Churches are not integrated. A food pantry is started. Interracial sports teams organized. We offer a summer film series for all God's children. For the first time in this town, black and white churches are in ministry together.

I also write letters for the editorial column of the local newspaper condemning racial prejudice, the injustice of capital punishment, and the neglect of the poor. Some folks are unhappy, fist-fight unhappy, especially a group of people outside the church. An outcry over my written remarks about racial prejudice and injustice sweeps the community.

I often hear racial remarks and slurs in the community. While out of town staying with her daughter, vandals strike a woman's house. A young black man is arrested for the break-in. When she returns home, I visit the woman in her home. She had every right to be angry and concerned. Someone violated her property and her personal space. The older lady who lived in the county for many years says to me, "I don't know what has happened to these white men around here. When I was a girl and something like this happened, the white men in the community would round up several of the black men, tie them to a tree, put axle grease on their heads, and pour white flour on them. We called it white-capping. It taught them a lesson."

Amusing incidents occur at church. Most pastors dislike officiating at weddings. Family dysfunctions rise to the surface as they often argue over time, place, and order. Rehearsals, ceremonies, and receptions stretch out over days, crippling pastors' weekend family time. Couples vow to be faithful, loving, and cherish one another for all time. Pastors know these promises often don't last long. One weekend, I officiate at a Saturday afternoon wedding. I dress in a dark suit, colorful yet conservative tie, but my new shiny black shoes hurt my feet. I plan to keep on bedroom shoes until I go out the door. Our dog chewed up my bedroom shoes. My kids bought me a pair of big, furry bedroom shoes as a gag gift for my birthday. I wear them because they are the only bedroom shoes I have at the time. All dressed except for the black shoes, I watch a football game on television, passionately involved. Checking my watch, it is time to depart for the church. Grabbing my jacket, I dash out the door and head to officiate at the ceremony. Just before the exchanging of vows and during a solo performed by a friend of the bride, I look down. My tie is straight and the pleats still in my trouser legs. Then I notice. I still have on the big, fluffy bedroom shoes. I receive lots of good nature teasing at the reception following the ceremony.

Large screws secure long wooden pews to the church sanctuary floor. Over time, the screws loosen. The pews are wobbly. The church has a committee that oversees the physical building and grounds. Susie, Royce, Alice, and Tom, all dedicated members of the committee, repair the pews one evening during the week. On Sunday morning, I proudly inform the congregation: "Susie and Royce, Alice and Tom were in the sanctuary earlier this week screwing in the pews." As fate would have it there are two women and two men I identify as "screwing in the pews." I notice some giggling in the congregation and a few polite elbow jabs that are meant to communicate "Did you hear what he said?" The verbal blunder does not dawn on me at the moment. Friends are happy to point it out later over lunch. Fortunately for me, this congregation had a good sense of humor.

About the same time, I invite an African-American family to a service of worship at church. I met them at an Interfaith gathering. They are new to the community and interested in our church. It is a brazen move. This is the 1980s, and segregation in the Old South is still as popular as donuts and coffee. On Monday morning, I am 'welcomed' as I arrive at my church office by a long line of cars and pickup trucks with farmers, merchants, and white people from all walks of life. They are not there to praise the work of Martin Luther King Jr. They tell me how unacceptable it is to invite "blacks" to church, how it would not be tolerated, and how it would end up with "blacks marrying our daughters." Saying "in seminary they taught me to invite all people to church," I try to side-step their hostility. I offer them seats in the sanctuary to talk about things. Instead, their leader says, "I think we got our point across." They grumble as they leave the church property. Later in the morning as I drive to a nearby city for a hospital visit, the local sheriff who is a friend of many in the crowd gathered at the church gets within inches of my rear bumper and escorts me to the county line. How far would the unhappy people go? Is there any danger to my family? I hope not.

The church rocked by the incident remains steady. One of the church members, the wealthiest man in the county, announces he is taking his family to a new church that "believes in the Bible." We worry our church finances will be crippled. Amazingly, contributions to the church rise above previous levels. Members are obviously determined to make up the difference as a statement of support.

Holy smokes, I almost started a "race war"! I wondered how well I handled the situation? Was I insensitive to the long-held and cherished "beliefs" of these, otherwise, fine citizens and church members? Did I move too quickly to integrate the church?

Pastoral demands and psychological crises of several church members stretch me to my limits. Betty (not her real name) comes into my office with tears running down her cheeks. I invite her to sit. She cries out "The world is so dark, coming to an end soon. I am going to die." I quickly reassure her I watched the morning news, and the world was not coming to an end. Didn't help. She describes how she cannot sleep at night, has loss of appetite, and cries a lot (all answers to diagnostic questions I would later learn to ask). I helped her some but probably only due to the re-assurance she felt from going to talk to her pastor.

A few days later, the phone rings. After identifying himself, Betty's psychiatrist thanks me for giving support to his patient. He shares with me what he thought I should know about Betty. As a child, she was sexually abused by an uncle who came into her bedroom in the dark of night. Betty, according to her psychiatrist, was suffering from panic attacks, intense but repressed rage, and near-psychotic breaks. "Angry enough to kill her abuser," he illuminated, "she has turned the rage in on herself."

Like a child at Disney World for the first time, I'm amazed at his insights and colorful explanations shedding so much light on this woman's intense pain and suffering. From that day forward, I am determined to learn how to understand people who come to see me in my office with their emotional needs.

I also realize I should not be functioning in such isolation in the small town church. Participating in a pastors' support group at the Virginia Institute of Pastoral Care proves blissfully helpful. Members of the group talk about their ministry situations and pastoral tribulations. A trained member of the institute facilitates the group. The institute is staffed by ordained clergy of all denominations. These women and men received advanced training and certification in pastoral counseling, a discipline integrating psychology and theology. Finding out about a part-time certificate program in pastoral counseling, I step on another slippery-slope and a change in pastoral identity from church pastor to a pastoral counselor.

The part-time program only partially satisfies my hunger for the diagnostic ability the above psychiatrist demonstrated. Soon, I apply to the full-time, two-year residency program in pastoral counseling. However, I'm told I need more "clinical experience" (apparently stopping the end of the world and starting a racial crisis is not enough). Consequently, I volunteer at a local mental health clinic.

My first client (an elderly man) sits down in his chair and says "I need your help . . . I've lost my nature." It takes me a few minutes to figure it out, but he wants help with his impotency. A colleague later tells me he has a client whose "presenting issue" was that he had "developed infancy."

The next client comes to the mental health clinic with her mother. The client in her early twenties has few relationships outside her family. Agitated and anxious, she relates to me with a great deal of suspicion. She glances at the door frequently as if she expects someone to come in. She talks about a neighbor who put a "spell" on her. She fears her mother might already be under a spell from the neighbor. After the session, I take my notes to the clinic consulting psychiatrist. "Schizotypal Personality Disorder" he says after hearing the symptomatology. Then he adds, "David, that's a tough start. Your first two cases: Impotency and Schizotypal Personality Disorder. Shame you can't just get a client with everyday run-of-the-mill depression or anxiety." Either sink or swim, I learn differential mental health diagnosis in real-time.

Soon, I have enough experience to qualify for the full-time residency program. VIPCare training stretches me emotionally, personally, and intellectually. It is easily one of the major formative events in my life. Studying the *Diagnostic and Statistical Manual for Mental Disorders (DSM-IV)*, abnormal psychology, the theology of pastoral counseling, theories of personality, and receiving intense supervision of my interaction with clients is exactly what I need (although sometimes I think "the world was coming to an end"). With great anxiety, I often push the play button for the recorded session with a client. My supervisor scrutinizes every word I say like a scientist peering through a microscope. Over time it is so helpful. After graduation, I serve on the staff at VIPCare for over fifteen years while developing a journal for clergy and conferences for clergy.

As a Licensed Professional Counselor (LPC) in Virginia, I was required to obtain twenty hours of continuing education per year. I enroll in courses provided by various mental health educational services approved by the licensing board in Virginia. The courses are on everything in the mental health field, from eating disorders to pharmacological medications for mental health disorders. One course is led by a psychologist who gave himself the title of "Dog Shit Psychologist." Boonford would love this guy! He explains how every client with a mental health disorder can be diagnosed by their reaction to stepping in dog shit. After stepping in a smelly pile, a person exclaims "This always happens to me. It is all I deserve," the person is diagnosed with depression. If a person reacts with "Oh God, I am ruined. My shoes will stink forever. People won't like me anymore. What am I going to do?" the person has an Anxiety Disorder. A person with a Paranoid Personality Disorder is immediately convinced it's a CIA plot. A psychotic person might be convinced the smelly, gooey substance on his shoes is radioactive material left behind by an alien spacecraft.

Triplets Born! Editor, Publisher, Convener

"Victory has a hundred fathers. Defeat is an orphan."

PRESIDENT JOHN F. KENNEDY

WHILE ENJOYING CONTINUING EDUCATION courses provided by teachers like Professor "Dog Poop" and continuing to be challenged by clients with every mental health disorder under the sun, I continue to preach occasionally. I do not preach every week, which affords me the opportunity to hear others preach, a luxury most pastors do not have. I notice few pastors are exposed to ideas and insights from the pastoral theology field (other than a basic seminary course). I introduce to our counseling institute staff the idea of publishing a newsletter that takes the scripture readings and illuminates them with the ideas and insights about the human condition from the field of pastoral theology. The staff liked the idea, but as I already knew, we were overworked already.

Should I try the project myself? In my spare time? Not that I have a lot. Intrigued, I ponder about a newsletter for pastors with pastoral implications of the lectionary texts for each Sunday. The lectionary is a set of biblical texts assigned to each Sunday of the year for preaching. The texts are assigned to the Sundays based on the theme of the season in the church year. Advent, for example, is assigned texts about John the Baptist while the Christmas season has texts about Jesus' birth.

I talk to pastors about the newsletter. One says, "You should have a Bible study (exegesis) article on the text as well." Another says, "If it is going to have an essay on the text from a pastoral theologian, how about an essay from a historical theologian? How has this text influenced the formation of doctrine in the life of the church?" And I wonder: Why not an essay from an art historian on how the text inspired art and literature? How about a section that reviews previously written sermons on the text? The newsletter would need a homiletical article ("a how-to" on constructing the sermon) written by a homiletics professor or a well-known preacher. (Homiletics is another name for preaching.) Added up that is six essays per week. The newsletter has become a monthly journal! It seemed like an incredible task but so energy generating and exciting!

Exegesis of Biblical Text—>Theological Themes—>Pastoral Implications—>Text and the Arts—>Sermon Reviews—>Preaching the Lesson

Manufacturing the courage, I take my idea to a former seminary professor in the biblical studies department of my seminary. Sitting in his office, I enthusiastically tell him about my project. He remains stone-faced. "Why doesn't he share my excitement?" I wonder. He speaks and crushes my dream. "This can't be done. It is too big of a project. You can't rely on people to get those essays to you on time." He kept naming reasons why my idea was doomed.

I thank him for his time and begin the drive home. In my mind, the painful memory emerges of my biological father saying to me when I was leaving for college that I was doomed to fail. It seemed like the same message the professor had just given me, although I suspected my professor was correct. Starting a publication from scratch would be an enormous project.

Still, I like the energy generated in me by the idea. I consult with some more people. One is my former pastoral care professor. "David, you don't have to be crazy to do this, but it might help." He said. A homiletics professor after hearing my proposal said "If you can pull this off, you will be inventing interdisciplinary exegesis." (Exegesis is a method of Bible interpretation taught in seminary that uses the tools of literary, historical, and source research.)

The vision of the publication before me, I "chomp at the bit" to do this. With five-hundred and fifteen dollars "to my name" I start *Lectionary Homiletics*, a monthly journal with six essays per week. I secure a biblical scholar, a theologian, a pastoral theologian, and an art history scholar to write an article on a text coming up in the lectionary a couple of months later. I write the first homiletical essay. The essays are stored on cassette tapes, using a primitive Radio Shack TRS-80 computer.

I pay the writers and pay a printing company to print several hundred copies. The sample issue is born. With the small amount of money left, I buy the mailing labels of two hundred pastors across the country.

On the floor of our living room, the children help me put on mailing labels. We mail the samples, along with a subscription form. But I'm now broke, not a penny left.

To my amazement, pastors mail in the subscription forms with checks! I use the money to buy more labels and mail more copies, oftentimes staying up all night to get them out. I am though in a bit of jeopardy. The paid subscribers expect a new preaching journal to arrive soon, but I have already spent their money on sending out more samples. If the journal doesn't materialize, I am probably guilty of fraud.

Fortunately, more subscription money arrives. *Lectionary Homiletics* is off to the races. I recruit the writers and edit each issue for twenty-five years. In the early years when the budget is tight, I not only recruit the writers and edit the monthly I also do the layout, edit the final version, get it to the printer, handle the advertising, and keep the financial books. The internet is born, and the publication goes digital as well. Several Christian publishing companies "borrow" my format and start similar publications.

I need six writers each week with each producing one thousand-word essays. Most writers accept the invitations to write. I purposely give them deadlines that are far ahead of when I actually need the essays. This is a life-saver because as my professor earlier warned "writers will often not get their essays to you on time." If I need essays in September, I give them a July deadline. By September, I usually have the essays.

My pastoral identity takes another shift. *Lectionary Homiletics* fast becomes nationally and internationally popular. Nothing like it exists at the time. Our website is *Goodpreacher.com.* Maybe the highest compliment paid to a pastor is "She is a good preacher." "Good preacher" means more than just good preaching. The term "good preacher" means she is appreciated for pastoral care, preaching, and the totality of ministry. On the other hand, when someone says, "the little preacher at the church on the corner," that pastor does not have a lot of respect.

Homiletical Hot Tub becomes one of the first preaching blogs (we-blog) on the internet. Various well-known preachers and professors are secured to help me post daily and timely "posts" on the biblical texts for the week.

In the office late in the afternoon when the small staff has departed for home, I often answer the phone and from time to time talk to some interesting people. One afternoon, the phone rings. The man says he wants to know if his subscription is about to expire. I ask his name. He answers, "Jeb Magruder." Seeing his name in the database, I ask "of . . . ?" Before I could finish my question, he says, "That's me, Watergate and all." Jeb Stuart Magruder was a special assistant to President Richard Nixon when the Watergate scandal went public. He was later convicted and spent several months in federal prison. After prison, he attended Princeton Seminary and became a pastor.

Another later afternoon, I answer the phone. A woman's voice is on the other end. She wants to change her address from her home to a P.O. box. She explains the Secret Service goes through all her mail and delays it by days, if not weeks, since the terrorist attack on 9/11. She is a pastor in northern Virginia but married to a high-ranking official in the White House in the George Bush administration.

Sitting at my desk one day, the phone rings. My assistant answers and says, "It's Dr. James Fowler of Emory University." I had extended him an invitation to write a series of articles. Dr. Fowler wrote an important book, *Stages of Faith*, along the lines of Eric Erickson's seminal work in psychology *Stages of Psycho-Social Development*. Fowler described six stages of faith development. I cannot recall how the connection was made that day on the phone, but we discovered we had both grown up near Boonford. Dr. Fowler's father was a United Methodist pastor assigned to Kona United Methodist Church, not far from Boonford. His stay in Kona was brief compared to my complete childhood in the area. After a few years, his father was transferred to another UMC church "off somewhere." We shared some similar memories on the phone that day. Young Fowler was fortunate to escape the theological clutches of Pastor Leroy.

I continue my work as a pastoral counselor, preach occasionally, and do my best to be a good husband and father, which meant I work all day, have family time, and then work at night when others sleep. The work though is so exciting and keeps me going.

After two years of editing and publishing *Lectionary Homiletics*, I hear from pastor-subscribers "we need a good preaching conference . . . why don't you start one?" From the counseling agency library, I borrow, for listening as I drive, a set of cassette tapes from The Evolution Conference of Psychotherapy sponsored by the Milton Erickson Foundation. The cassette tapes are the lectures and debates from this gathering of famous psychologists and psychotherapists in Phoenix each year.

The Evolution Conference of Psychotherapy each year brought together the great theorists from psychology. In a confrontational format, B.F. Skinner might give a lecture on behavioral therapy and why behavioral therapy was the best modality for therapists to use in treating clients. Then a response to the lecture would be given from a person from the opposite end of the psychological theory spectrum. For instance, Carl Rogers, who had no interest in behavioral therapy, but was a strong advocate of client-centered (feelings and relationship) therapy, would give a response. Often verbal fireworks erupt between the two presenters as they defend their views. Then a panel would discuss with the two all the implications of what they had just heard. We were stimulated by the interaction.

It occurred to me if there was going to be a preaching conference, this would be the model: presenter, responder from a different theoretical viewpoint, and a panel. I took the idea to a homiletics professor at Union Theological Seminary. To my surprise, she embraced the idea. She offered to help secure speakers. Even more surprising, Tom Long, Nora Tubbs Tisdale, David Buttrick, Jim Forbes, Jana Childers, and many other highly respected figures in the field of homiletics agreed to speak.

Yet, another shift in pastoral identity begins. The *Festival of Homiletics* makes its debut during the third week of May in 1992 in Williamsburg, Virginia. By design, I do not have to travel far. Surprisingly nearly five hundred pastors from all over the United States register to attend. Maybe they just want to visit Williamsburg? Incredibly anxious the entire week, I catastrophize in my mind about all the things that could go wrong. What if the pastors are gravely disappointed? What if the electricity fails? What if the next speaker does not show up? What if? What if?

Held in a hotel ballroom, the *Festival of Homiletics* is a rousing success, thanks to the graciousness and shared wisdom of so many people. At the end of the week, pastors approach me and ask "Where is this going to be next year?" Surprised by the interest, I say, "What? Next year?" I haven't thought about next yet, thinking it might be a one-time event. But I promise the pastors I will start working on it.

For *Festival of Homiletics* 1994, I secure an auditorium at the University of North Carolina at Wilmington, close to the beach, and an additional drawing card (I hope). I invite Barbara Brown Taylor (Episcopal priest and *New York Times* best-selling author) to speak. The *Festival of Homiletics* still doesn't have "two nickels to rub together." I scrape for the financial resources to keep it going. Consequently, I place the speakers in dormitory rooms I rent from the university. Dorm rooms I had never seen (big mistake). This is before the day of nicely adorned dormitory rooms.

Barbara approaches me after her first night and says "David have you seen the room YOU put me in?" I mumbled out something, but it was not adequate.

"Well, tell me where you are staying?" She asks.

"Down on the beach, you see I have kids with me, and this is our vacation too." I respond.

Barbara is still not happy saying something like "No one has ever put me in a room like this one."

When writing the original manuscript for this book, I thought it might be a good idea to ask Barbara to take a look at what I had written about her. She responded ". . . the dorm room at UNC Wilmington had no telephone, no trash can, no towels, no curtains over the windows, and sheets that a night shelter would have rejected as too slick and full of polyester leprosy. A monastery, indeed . . ."

The next morning at the *Festival of Homiletics* in 1994, Barbara approaches me. I brace myself emotionally. She says, "David, I have reframed this experience. I'm seeing it as a retreat in a monastery. You know, just bare existence, good for the soul. Thank you." For sure, it was an experience of undeserved grace. I continue inviting Barbara for years, and to my surprise, she accepts most of the time until reaching retirement age and cutting back on her schedule.

The following year the *Festival of Homiletics* travels to Atlanta. One of many festivals held in Atlanta over the years. Once again the *Festival of Homiletics* is held in a hotel ballroom. The *Festival of Homiletics* is invited the next year to the National City Christian Church in Washington DC, the national church for the Disciples of Christ. It was the home-church of Lyndon Johnson while he was president. A pew still has his name on it. This begins a long tradition of having the *Festival of Homiletics* in a church.

The *Festival of Homiletics* evolves in other ways. The confrontational format based on The Evolution Conference of Psychotherapy worked well for psychotherapists, but homiletics professors and preachers are highly invested in being nice to each other. So I switch to a less confrontational format: sermons, lectures, workshops. I learn so much from the attending pastors. I recall early on a pastor coming up to me and saying "We need a good printed program for this event." Up until that time, we had a few handouts which were all that we could afford.

Remembering my background in psychotherapy, I organize seminars around the country for pastors in addition to the *Festival of Homiletics*. I bring in psychologists to help pastors be better equipped to deal with parishioners who come to them with emotional and mental health issues. Donald Meichenbaum, PhD, is one of the founders of cognitive behavior therapy and was voted one of the most influential psychologists of the twentieth century. Dr. Meichenbaum was a Professor of Clinical Psychology at the University of Waterloo in Toronto. To escape the cold in Canada, he spent the winter in Clearwater, Florida. He agreed to provide a workshop in neighboring Tampa for pastors on dealing with trauma and Post Traumatic Stress Disorder. The Oklahoma City bombing generated a lot of anxiety in parishioners that pastors had to deal with. After the workshop, Donald invites me to his condo overlooking the white beaches of Clearwater. So there I am, a poor emotionally impoverished boy-man from Boonford sharing a glass of wine with one of the leading psychologists in the world, although I doubt Pastor Leroy would be impressed.

For the *Festival of Homiletics*, attendees encourage me to invite Garrison Keillor, at the time the host of the wildly popular *A Prairie Home Companion* and called by many the best storyteller in America. Personally, I found great enjoyment on a Saturday early evening, sitting under a shade tree, and listening to the show. One of Keillor writers is also a part-time writer for *Lectionary Homiletics*, offering an occasional article on the Bible lesson for the week from the perspective of "the arts." The writer tells me Garrison often jokes that his radio program is like "church" with lots of music and that his monologue is like a sermon. For many years, I invite Garrison to speak, but his schedule prevents it. After a rejection one year, I suggest to his scheduler that I come to St. Paul (MN) and interview him. This could be done at a time of his choosing, and we would play the interview on a big screen at the *Festival of Homiletics*. Surprisingly, he accepts. We schedule a date which he cancels as the date approaches. Another date is scheduled and canceled as well.

Finally, a date in February does not get canceled. In Virginia the day of my flight to Minneapolis, the temperature is in the low seventies with bright, warming sunshine. I fail to check the weather forecast for Minneapolis-St Paul. Upon arriving at the airport, I notice the winds whipping outside. It is ten degrees above zero while the sky is clear brilliant blue. I am not dressed for the cold. Stepping outside to grab a cab, bitter winter winds slap my face. The interview is the next day, so I check into my downtown hotel on that Sunday evening.

Looking for a good restaurant, I walk down streets, stunned by the cold. I find an open restaurant down a side street and enjoy a fine dinner of grilled Walleye, boiled potatoes, and red pickled cabbage. The server warns me it is dangerously cold outside, minus ten degrees with a frightful wind blowing making the wind-chill close to thirty degrees below zero!

Leaving the diner, I turn left toward my hotel. The problem is that my hotel is to the right! I walk and walk but no hotel. A late Sunday evening, all the buildings downtown are closed. I continue walking, not realizing, in the wrong direction. A neon light on a building shows minus twelve degrees. Back in Virginia, my hat and winter coat would be sufficient for any winter weather but not here. The severe cold penetrates through my clothes and into my body. My chest feels like it is about to explode from the cold. My head throbs intensely. It dawns on me that I am in big trouble because all the buildings are locked and I do not see the welcoming lights of my hotel. I realize I went the wrong way, reverse my path, and just in time make it back to the hotel. Barely able to breathe from the tightening of my chest, I stumble into the lobby where attendants help me to a sofa and put warming blankets over me. Fortunately this evening, there will not be news back in Boonford that another Howell has perished and gone the way of Pastor Leroy's curse.

Up early the next morning, a taxi takes me across the Mississippi River to St Paul. The offices for *A Prairie Home Companion* are in an old radio station, a series of one-story buildings joined together, and on one end is a towering radio tower. The tower and station are non-functioning, but the building provides adequate office space for the staff. The recording crew I have hired arrive at the appointed hour, but Garrison Keillor is not to be seen. We wait an hour. A half-hour later, he arrives. I introduce myself. Beneath the bushy eyebrows, Keillor's eyes intensely stare at me. It is only seconds but felt like hours. Internally, I say to myself, "Oh no! He knows now I am not a well-read man. That I don't read the poetry of Walt Whitman or any poet. He already knows my intellect is simple and limited." I wonder to myself, "Will he finally grant me the interview?"

Garrison says, "Let's get started." What follows is a fascinating conversation. He grew up in a fundamentalist family in small-town Minnesota. He was in church three times per week and knows the Bible almost by heart. Now, he is an Episcopalian and (like me) has escaped the clutches of fundamentalism.

How he prepares his monologues is of great interest to pastors. He says he begins his monologues with "It's been a quiet week in Lake Wobegon" because he wants to keep the listeners' expectations low, so as not to disappoint. I am interested in his storytelling technique and how it might inform sermon writing. He describes how he takes a normal event in the life of *Lake Wobegon*, spins it into a crisis with increasing tension and drama, and finally a pleasing climax and resolution.

On another trip to Minneapolis for a *Festival of Homiletics*, I fly into Chicago a day early and catch a train to South Bend, Indiana. A dream of mine is to attend a football game at Notre Dame and experience the Touchdown Jesus thing with the statue of Jesus towering on the field in the back of one end zone. Sitting beside me on the train, a man explains he is going to the game as well but will first visit with his daughter. She is a member of the Notre Dame band that will perform at half-time. Additionally, the rock band *Chicago* will perform with them at half-time. Since we are arriving well before game time, he invites me to the rehearsal in a courtyard on the Notre Dame campus.

We arrive first. A few other parents of band members gather as well. Then *Chicago* enters the courtyard. We watch as they take horns and guitars out of carrying cases. We stand forty feet away, but the entrance is behind us. As more parents and friends enter, we have to move closer to the front and *Chicago*. A large space is reserved behind where *Chicago* stands, and promptly the Notre Dame band marches in and fills the spot. Friends and parents keep filling the courtyard behind us. We are pushed closer and closer to *Chicago*. When they begin to play, we are ten feet from the famous band. When they play, their horns are deafening. It feels like my hair is being blown backward from the close intensity of the music, but it is thrilling to be so close to fame. To this day, I blame *Chicago* for my tinnitus, the constant roaring in my ears.

Since it is a night game and the huge crowd slow in exiting the stadium, I miss the last train to Chicago. It is past midnight. I walk around South Bend and down side streets. Taxi drivers have all gone home. I stumble into a police station. I explain my plight to one of the officers and ask if there are any buses to Chicago that time of night. The officers laugh. One officer says, "I'm getting off at 2:00 AM. I'll take you to Chicago. We want visitors in our town to have a good experience." I was duly impressed and fortunate. On the way, the station on the car radio plays *"25 or 6 to 4"* by *Chicago*. A lot of folks think the song is about drugs, but according to Robert Lamm, organist who wrote the song, it's about late-night song writing. For me at that moment, the song was about early morning police car riding.

One of my writers for *Lectionary Homiletics* is a Catholic priest, Father Al. He teaches at a school in New York and is also the Catholic chaplain for the Indy Car Racing Series. His summers are spent following the Indy series around the country. Many of the drivers are Catholic, and he provides a private Holy Communion service for many of the families before the races.

Father Al invites me to an Indy race. Thrilled to accept, I meet him hours before race time at the main gate and before regular ticket holders can enter. He guides me through the gate and past security. We hop on his golf cart, go into the race track, into the infield, and through a tunnel. We arrive at a large green grassy area behind the track and the towering stands. Nestled in the grass are RVs. Some RVs are connected by large white tents. The RVs provide housing for the drivers and their families. The tents are dining areas with rows of tables and chairs. Father Al says, "David, let's eat before I provide Holy Communion for the drivers." We enter a tent where a few people are already seated. They all recognize Father Al. He directs me to sit toward one end of a row of tables. Cold items are already on the table. In a few minutes, servers bring in pans of pasta, meats, and vegetables. There are a few empty chairs around us. A husband and wife take a seat beside me. It is Michael Andretti. We chat with him over dinner, and Andretti invites us into the infield for the race. Track-side he has a booth with several computers. When the race starts, he and a technician monitor the race car driven by his son, Marco Andretti. Father Al and I leave the booth. In front of us is Ashley Judd who was married to driver Dario Franchitti. Ashley and Father Al have become friends.

A few years into the *Festival of Homiletics*, several attending pastors said "You must get Reverend Otis Moss to preach." I set out to find Otis Moss, and I find him in Augusta GA. Before email, I send a letter. Quickly, I receive an enthusiastic affirmative response. The festival is in Chicago with Otis Moss scheduled to speak on Wednesday afternoon. After lunch, a striking, handsome, and young man approaches me and introduces himself as Otis Moss III. In a short time, several of the pastors who recommended Otis Moss tell me, "You got the wrong Otis Moss . . . that's his son . . . he just got out of seminary . . . you were supposed to get Otis Moss, Jr. from Cleveland!" Well, Otis Moss III steps to the podium that afternoon and rocked the house. The rest is history. Otis is always listed in the top ten preachers lists in America. I often say I discovered Otis Moss, but it would have been a small matter of time before the prophetic voice of Otis Moss III is heard near and far.

Fourth Presbyterian Church in Chicago hosts the festival several times. The "Magnificent Mile" is a wonderful place for pastors to dine and relax between sessions. Pastor Jeremiah Wright of Trinity United Church of Christ later becomes infamous for his remarks about the United States. Most pastors I know believe he was misquoted and misunderstood. Before the political incident, I invite Pastor Wright to bring his choir and preach at an evening of worship at Fourth Presbyterian Church. Fourth Presbyterian Church is a large, spacious church with a choir "loft" that I estimated would seat over one-hundred choir members. The service is to begin at 7:30 PM. Buses carrying Trinity United Church of Christ choir members start arriving at 7:20 PM. One bus pulls up in front of Fourth Presbyterian Church, then another, another, and another! The first person out of the bus is the music director/choir director sporting striking dread-locks. He begins singing and swaying. One by one choir members step off the buses singing and swaying. In sets of two, they march, sing, and sway into the sanctuary. The mostly white pastors in the pews join them in singing and swaying. But I have a huge problem! The choir area seats maybe one-hundred and twenty-five people. I estimate two-hundred and fifty choir members, if not more, are marching into the sanctuary. Body gripping anxiety sweeps over me. Pastor Wright and I quickly confer and ask the first four rows of pastors to move to the back, most have to stand. The pastors are happy to do so in order to get this electrifying choir into the front of the sanctuary.

Someone along the way suggests to me the most prophetic preachers of modern history might well have been in the leadership of the civil rights movement. I invite Reverend Andrew Young, close assistant of Martin Luther King Jr, to speak. Reverend Joseph Lowery is also invited. Lowery, highly involved with the Freedom Riders, founded the Southern Leadership Conference, and has a street named after him in Atlanta. He also gave the benediction at President Obama's first inauguration.

An interesting exchange occurs with Reverend Lowery while he waits to speak at the *Festival of Homiletics* in Nashville. Backstage, we talk for over an hour. When the civil rights movement starts and when he joins Dr. King's movement, he is a United Methodist pastor in Alabama. When Governor George Wallace finds out about his involvement in the Civil Rights movement, Wallace confiscated all of Dr. Lowery's personal property, even his car. His friends go to the auction and buy his car back for him.

Lowery admits the civil rights activists, even Dr. King, became discouraged enough to quit. The struggle seems like too big of a mountain to climb with so much resistance to change. The powers that are opposed to them have the police on their side. Their marches are being met with brutal force from the police who should be protecting them. Then Lowery said, "But Aretha wrote that song." Lowery pauses as he could see I'm thinking, "What song?" After a few moments, he says "RESPECT, the song hit us like a cannonball of inspiration. That's all we wanted RESPECT. It became our anthem." Aretha's song went to number one on the charts and stayed there for twelve weeks.

Lowery continued telling me these incredible stories. After George Wallace is no longer governor and confined to a wheelchair, Ted Turner invites Lowery, Wallace, and several other prominent figures to Atlanta for interviews about the civil rights movement. Reverend Lowery is the first one to arrive at the studio. Sitting on one side of the room, he sees former Governor Wallace in his wheelchair coming through the door on the other side of the room and toward him. As he gets closer, Reverend Lowery sees tears coming down former Governor Wallace's face. When he gets to Reverend Lowery, Wallace tearfully says, "Reverend Lowery, I am sorry for what I did to you." Remarkable indeed!

Better music becomes another request from the attendees. I recruit some top-flight musicians. One of those musicians, Beth Nielsen Chapman had been to South Africa and performed at an event where Nobel Peace prize winner Archbishop Desmond Tutu was the featured speaker. They became great friends. Beth agreed to help secure the Archbishop for the *Festival of Homiletics*. Reverend Lowery, Andrew Young, and others agreed to write letters to the Archbishop.

Incredibly, Archbishop Desmond Tutu agrees to speak at the festival in Atlanta. The hotel where the Archbishop would be staying offers to provide a passenger van to pick up the Archbishop, his wife, and an assistant at the airport. The hotel gives me permission to travel in the van as well. In the past, there were threats against the Archbishop's life. Several weeks before the Archbishop arrives, I alert TSA at the airport that the Archbishop is coming and ask them to make arrangements to get him through security as quickly as possible. TSA blunders the whole thing and does not show up in time. The Archbishop just goes through the airport like any other person, shaking hands as he went.

In the van going back to the hotel, I sit in the back with the Archbishop. We talk about several things.

"We are forecast to have great weather this week. The *Festival of Homiletics* is fortunate every year in that regard. I can't remember when we had rain the week of the festival." I say proudly.

With a puzzled look on his face, the Archbishop says "David, where I am from, we have a gathering, and it rains on us, we feel blessed!" Obviously, I am still working on cultural awareness.

Oh Brother, Pass The Pork Bellies!

"The family is one of nature's masterpieces."

GEORGE SANTAYANA

AT AN ATLANTA CONFERENCE, I fuse together my past and present. My brother, Larry Howell, tells me about a fabulous African-American choir near Boonford at Griffin Chapel, an AME Zion congregation. I preview a couple of recordings and ask my brother to invite them to Atlanta to perform when Archbishop Tutu speaks. A choir from a small isolated African-American church in the Appalachian Mountains and a Nobel Peace Prize winner from South Africa blending together beautifully. Who would have 'thunk' it?

My brother also brings to light an interesting piece of Burnsville history that not one soul in Burnsville knew about. He drives home from Johnson City, Tennessee one afternoon, listening to the radio. The station plays songs by the famous Carter family (Maybelle, AP, June), and then plays a song by Lesley Riddle. The announcer says Riddle was from Burnsville, North Carolina. My brother begins a two-year research project into the life and influence of the talented musician. Lesley Riddle (1905–1975), an African-American resident of the Higgins community in Burnsville, had a role in the shaping of country music in America.

At fifteen, Riddle, working in a cement plant, loses his left leg just below the knee cap. Unable to work for some time, he plays his guitar until his fingers bleed. His musical skills soar. AP Carter hears Lesley Riddle play a guitar and is so impressed he invites him to his home in Mace Springs, Virginia. Victor Records had just released AP and Maybelle Carter's first album, and they needed new material. Lesley teaches Maybelle how to play a sliding guitar using a pocket-knife, and he taught her a song that makes her famous, "The Cannon Ball." For six years starting in 1931, the amazing Lesley Riddle and AP Carter tour the upper South, learning and playing songs of each area. Many of these songs are passed down to their daughter, June Carter Cash and her husband of much fame, Johnny. Romance takes Lesley to Rochester, New York, where he dies. Many of the Carter family attend his funeral. On information shared with him by my brother, Ken Burns, in his documentary (*PBS*) on the history of country music, pays tribute to Lesley Riddle. Burnsville now has an annual RiddleFest each summer. Many of Lesley Riddle's relatives are in the choir singing with the Nobel Peace Prize winner Archbishop Desmond Tutu at the *Festival of Homiletics*.

Another year in Atlanta, Peachtree Road United Methodist Church in-house chef fixes us breakfast and lunch every day. Appreciative of the hard work of the chef, I say to him about mid-week, "I want to take you out to dinner. You have been so gracious to us this week, and we really appreciate it. And I want you to pick the restaurant." I figured as a chef he knows the Atlanta restaurant scene. Did he ever! He takes us to a restaurant at Atlanta's most expensive hotel.

I invite several of the speakers and musicians to join us for dinner, along with my brother who makes it down from the mountains of North Carolina to help with the festival. When we are seated at the restaurant, I say to Al, the chef, "I want you to order appetizers for us." Sounds like I was being wonderfully gracious, but again I figured he knew the good stuff. As a foodie, motives are rarely pure.

Chef Al orders the appetizers. First out are pork bellies, just coming on the food scene then. Pork bellies are nothing more than a different kind of bacon cut. When I am growing up in Western North Carolina, we raise "a hog" every year, and that's how we feed ourselves in the cold winter months when we didn't have vegetables. We eat cheap bacon (pork bellies) not because we like it that much but because we have it.

Sitting at the pricy restaurant in Atlanta with some world-class musicians and big city/high-steepled preachers, my brother starts laughing, loud enough to be heard across the restaurant. He slaps me on the back. He says "Little brother, do you realize the irony of this?" I am not as smart as my brother, so I have to say sheepishly "No," wondering what I'm missing.

He says: "Remember when you were young and each fall after the killin' of the hog and after you ate the cheap fatty bacon for weeks you vowed to move away, get a good education and job, so you wouldn't have to eat that stuff anymore?" Oh, the irony!

Another incident demonstrated to me the cultural and cuisine differences between my childhood and the lives of my children. Several times a year, I take our teenagers Wendy and Meredith and nine-year-old son Morgan, to the mountains of North Carolina to visit their grandmother and other relatives. One trip we visit for their first time their great aunts, Maggie and Bessie Howell, both "spinsters" near ninety. They live where the road ends. Sam Greene Road is a seldom-used side road off Arbuckle Road in Yancey County. Beyond their house is all wilderness. They live in a 1800s log cabin with Panther Ridge in the background. "Granny" played by Irene Ryan on the *Beverly Hillbillies* reminded me of Maggie, while Bessie was more like Ma Joad in *Grapes of Wrath*.

They heat their log cabin with wood the entire year, no matter the temperature outside. Out of the chimney blue-gray smoke curls toward the sky as we arrive. Chickens chase each other in the yard. The yard is dirt, packed down by over two hundred years of footsteps. We step inside the log cabin. My daughters' eyes start to pop out of their heads. Inside is take-your-breath-away hot. The floor probably hasn't been swept in years. Water running by gravity from a spring on Panther Mountain drips rapidly from a faucet. Oil lamps burn. They don't want electricity, doing just fine, thank you!

The log cabin interior consists of one large room with a woodstove, sink, table, chairs, and two small beds. The other room is locked. Rumor circulates their father's clothes still hang in that room, apparently a shrine since he died over fifty years ago. Smells of sweat and urine greet us. A sand-colored cat jumps from Bessie's lap and curls up on a small well-worn rug.

The great aunts politely spit out their remaining snuff into an old coffee can and wipe the snuff juice residue from the corners of their mouths before they hug us. Tiny wire-rim glasses sit on the end of their noses. Hair is gathered in buns on the back of their heads. Dresses fall to their ankles. Thrilled to have a visit, they invite us to sit. In short sleeves and shorts, our skin sticks to soiled, ancient wooden chairs. On the mantle, a stunning wooden clock, probably a cherished antique, ticks and tocks the seconds of remaining life away.

The great aunts are keenly interested in the two young women from a far city. The ancient women ask what grade they are in and if they have boyfriends? A pot of pinto beans boils on the woodstove. "Stay for dinner and have some pintos and cornbread with us!" Bessie offers. "I'll even fix you some cornbread and milk."

On the other side of the dirt road reside the only neighbors. Insects buzz and chirp as we cross the road. Sadie and Earl live a hard life, living off the land. Their skin is tortured, scaly brown from the sun. Their backs hunched from working in fields sunup to sundown. A grandson lives with them. On this Saturday morning, they make sorghum molasses. Sugar cane does not grow in the mountains, but sorghum grass, which also makes fine molasses, grows well at the high elevations. Outside fires roar with big pots of boiling water hanging from homemade tripods. This is an oversimplification, but the sorghum grass is boiled until it is reduced to juice and finally to molasses. The smells of smoky burning wood and the sweet sorghum boiling mixture fill the air this clear summer morning. Crows caw loudly in the distance as we walk toward their little farm. The tops of tall pine trees, watching over this two house village for over a century, gently sway in the soft breeze.

The grandson and my son are about the same nine-year age. The young mountaineer drinks a yellow liquid from a mason quart jar. I ask him what he's drinking. He says with a big glowing smile, "Oh, that's the juice left-over from a jar of pickled corn. Grandma saves it for me." He wants to show us the barn and the farm animals. We smell rotting straw as the grandson points proudly to his hogs and milk cows. Beside the barn sits a wood-framed cage with mesh wire around it. "How do you like my fat white rabbit?" he asks as he points to the cage. Before anyone can answer, he adds, "We had two rabbits last week." Wendy asks, "What happened to the other rabbit?" Without hesitation, the young man declares, "We ate it!" Both daughters run, screaming, to the car.

Festival of Homiletics attendees encourage me to attend the National Storytelling Festival held in Jonesborough, TN, in October of each year. Historic Jonesborough, the oldest town in Tennessee, delights thousands of storytelling attendees with quaint old buildings, craft-art shops, and welcoming restaurants. Glistening white tents with two thousand folding chairs in each are erected in every available patch of ground in this little town. To my surprise, many of the popular storytellers are preachers. The most popular storyteller is Donald Davis, a United Methodist minister, and now a full-time storyteller. Two-thousand fans pack his tent with more standing around the edges of the tent, leaning in to hear his every word. Stunned, I hear him telling stories of growing up in the mountains of North Carolina in a little town called Waynesville. For twenty or more years, my efforts were to avoid telling people I was from the mountains of North Carolina. The two thousand plus listeners treasure every word as Donald tells them about odd and unusual mountain folk. I remind myself I could never tell stories like Donald Davis, but I have lived stories just like he tells.

Many of the speakers for the *Festival of Homiletics* supply wonderful encouragement over the years. Will Willimon of Duke University, Anna Carter Florence of Columbia Seminary, Tom Long of Emory University, Barbara Brown Taylor, Walter Brueggemann, Bishop Yvette Flunder, Michael Curry, David Lose, Brian McLaren, and many others implore me to "keep up the great work." They offer names of talented young speakers.

During a summer vacation in Europe, I hear a concert by a Chopin pianist from Poland. After his concert, we have a conversation. He agrees to play at the next festival. I pay for his travel, room and board, but it will be a surprise treat for the festival attendees. Introducing a novel performance (musician, storyteller, poet, novelist, etc.) keeps the *Festival of Homiletics* innovative and interesting.

In a few years, attendees suggest I invite Peter Mayer to play at the event.

"Who is Peter Mayer?" I ask.

"He's Jimmy Buffett's lead guitarist." They say.

"Isn't that the band that sings 'Why Don't We Get Drunk and Screw?'" I inquire.

It didn't seem like a good fit to me, but they explain "He's not like Jimmy. His parents were missionaries in India, and when not touring with Jimmy, he likes to play for church events."

So I look into Peter Mayer and find a guy about as wholesome as they come: son of missionaries, home-schooled his kids, and a vegetarian. So we enjoy having Peter play at the *Festival of Homiletics* when he is not on the road with Buffett. Several times over the years, Peter extended me tickets and backstage passes to their concerts all up and down the east coast. One September, we flew to Paris and dined with Peter and the Coral Reefers before their concert at La Cigale/La Boule Noire.

In Minneapolis one year, we complete the Monday evening program and several of us go to the Dakota Jazz Club for a late dinner. A musician plays.

A person in our group says to me, "Do you know who that is?"

"No," I say.

She says with excitement in her voice "That's Les McCann."

I knew the name, associated with big events like The Grammys.

For his last song, he performs an incredible version of "Amazing Grace" with not a dry eye in the house. I am so moved I say to Rina, "You can talk jazz with him. Try to make your way backstage and see if he will sing that for us tomorrow at the festival?"

"Really?" she says.

"Yes," I said, "That was incredible. Offer him $1500."

After a long time backstage, Rina emerges "We talked a lot of jazz, and he would love to sing tomorrow, but he's scheduled to fly out in the morning. He lives in LA."

I say, "Go back and catch him before he leaves. Tell him we'll pay for a new flight."

He agrees. The next day, Les McCann plays piano and sings "Amazing Grace" and for many of over two thousand pastors tears run down their faces. An attendee comes up to me afterwards and says, "I didn't know Les McCann was going to be here." I said, "I didn't either."

While lining up musicians for the *Festival of Homiletics*, I met an incredible array of talented artists. When I see a musician performing in the area that might be a good fit with the *Festival of Homiletics*, I find a way, sometimes through an agent and at other times through my own initiative, to meet the band or the musician backstage. Sweet Honey in the Rock, an acapella group that performed at Carnegie Hall and The John F. Kennedy Center for the Performing Arts, is one of the first groups performing for us. I take my twelve-year-old son with me to visit backstage with the Blind Boys of Alabama. I forget to tell him they are all visually impaired. Shocked at first, he soon recovers.

Music agents often unload concert tickets and backstage passes they don't plan to use. An agent offered me tickets and backstage passes for the Beach Boys in Virginia Beach. The Beach Boys liked beer and shared the ups and downs of their sometimes erratic but very successful music career. While in Chicago, another agent handed me tickets to Wrigley Field to see the Chicago Cubs play. I did not realize how fortunate I was until we got to our seats directly behind home plate!

The *Festival of Homiletics* establishes a relationship with several Nashville-based singer/songwriters. Ashley Cleveland and Beth Chapman are accomplished musicians and songwriters for some of the best artists in Nashville. When the festival is in Nashville (every 3 years or so), Ashley and Beth organize "songwriters in the round" for evening entertainment. They sit in a semi-circle with guitars and take turns introducing their songs before they play them. It is interesting hearing how the songs are "born" out of their experiences.

Beth shares an interesting story. A famous multi-Grammy winning musician invites her to Texas to help him write a song. He lives on a ranch where Beth arrives after flying into the local airport. The next morning, the famed musician explains he and his friends like to play a round of golf before turning their attention to songwriting. He invites Beth to join. She agrees. At the first tee, the Texas musician says they like to wager a little money. She agrees to that as well. With eighteen holes in the book, Beth collects several thousand dollars in wagered money. She then confesses to the musician, "I didn't tell you I went to LSU on a golf scholarship."

In Nashville, one year to make arrangements for the festival coming up in a few months, one of our musicians invites me to the Loveless Cafe. The cafe is like the famed Blue Bird Cafe where singer/songwriters gather and perform spontaneously. The Loveless Cafe this evening has a structured format with several musicians playing. My friend plays last. My flight is late. By the time I arrive at the cafe (a large music hall serving food and beverages) several musicians have finished their sets. I notice a man with long, mostly gray, hair sitting on the front row with an attractive young woman. I forget about the couple and enjoy the music. When the evening music is over, I stay in my seat until the audience departs. I go to the door of the performers' dressing room and wait for my friend to come out. The door swings open. Alongside my friend is the gray-haired man and the young woman. My friend and I exchange greetings. Then he says, "David, this is Robert Plant." Robert Plant is there to hire my friend for a new band he is forming. For a few minutes, I talk to Robert Plant, the lead singer for the iconic rock band Led Zeppelin. I learn that the name Led Zeppelin was used out of fear the band might drop like a lead balloon. Just a few years ago, a major music publication ranked Led Zeppelin as the number one rock band of all time.

At a jazz supper club in Richmond, I hear a fantastic sixteen-year old jazz saxophone player Grace Kelly. I approach her father/manager about playing at the next *Festival of Homiletics*. She dazzles the audience at several festivals. I suggest to them she should record a CD of jazz hymns. They ask me to provide the "liner notes." I tried not to look embarrassed when I asked them what liner notes were (a description of the music and purpose of the CD on the inside jacket of the CD). Grace has gone on to play on The Late Show hosted by Stephen Colbert and with such musical notables as Wynton Marsalis. She played the national anthem before a Boston Celtics basketball game.

I bring in speakers from other disciplines to talk to the pastors about culture and preaching. Pulitzer Prize winner Leonard Pitts talks to us about systemic racism and political corruption. Noted environmentalist Bill McKibben presented a lecture on climate change. Former US poet laureate Natasha Trethewey shares with us through her poetry the difficulty of growing up in a bi-racial family in Mississippi and the trauma of having a mother murdered. Old Testament theologian Walter Bruggemann once told us, "Listen to the poets. They will be the first to tell us the truth about things."[9]

After 9/11, our office receives almost daily emails and letters from Pakistan and other countries in that area of the world. Each wants us to send them a letter of invitation to the *Festival of Homiletics* so they might obtain a visa from the U.S. State Department. I check with a friend working for the state department. As I suspect, he warns me about sending the letters. So I ignore the requests.

One day, I receive a phone call from a man who says he is a pastor in India and needs a letter of invitation for obtaining a visa. I explain I have been informed by the state department not to do that. He insists he wants to attend the festival so that he can learn how it operates and then establish a preaching festival in India. I wish him well and tell him if he gets a visa I will give him a complimentary registration.

I did not hear again from the pastor in India. In a few months, the *Festival of Homiletics* goes on as planned. On Wednesday as I often did, I dismiss the attendees for lunch. My back is turned from the speakers' area while I gather some notes from a table.

A voice behind me in non-American English, "Dawid, Dawid!"

I turn, not recognizing the man I say, "Can I help you?"

He says, "It's Sadhu from India. Remember me?"

Embarrassed I say, "No."

He explains we talked on the phone and I told him he could attend if he got a visa. I remember. We talk and laugh. I tell him we are excited to have him, but the conference started on Monday. He explains he flew into New York on Monday morning. Not being familiar with transportation in the United States, he spent days on various Greyhound buses finally making his way to Minneapolis after mistakenly going to Atlanta.

Church of England representatives visit the festival one year. They want to start a festival of preaching in England. We assist them with their planning. It seems the Brits need help with their preaching as well.

No pastor wanting to attend the *Festival of Homiletics* was turned away because of inability to pay. I extend to them a complimentary registration and ask them to help with the on-site registration. We also give refunds to pastors who had emergencies in their congregations and were unable to attend. Six months after a festival, a pastor calls. My assistant asks me to talk to him. He paid and is all prepared to attend the festival when he is in an automobile accident. Six months later, he is awake from a deep coma. I tell this Lazarus-pastor we will refund his conference fee and give him a complimentary conference registration for the next festival.

Atlanta establishes itself as a great city for the *Festival of Homiletics*. Peachtree Road United Methodist Church in upscale Buckhead is always a great host church with over 1500 seats and an enthusiastic staff to support us. The festival also used First Presbyterian Church and Ebenezer Baptist Church in Atlanta.

My first site visit to Ebenezer Baptist Church takes me on an unexpected journey. The Reverend Joseph L. Roberts, Jr. pastors at the time, having succeeded Dr. Martin Luther King, Jr. Ebenezer Baptist Church seats over 2000 people. The new church building is not the church where Reverend Martin Luther King, Jr. preached. He preached in the smaller historic Ebenezer Baptist Church across the street where the church offices remain. The new church was built after his death.

My appointment to meet with Reverend Roberts is scheduled at 11:00 AM. Arriving a few minutes early, his secretary informs me Reverend Roberts is helping officiate at a funeral that began at 10:00 AM. I cannot remember the name now, but the service is for a prominent Civil Rights activist. At 12:30 PM, I am told that the service is about half completed because there are a number of notable speakers who have come in from around the country.

The secretary introduces me to a man about sixty years of age. He is going to show me around the area by car until the funeral concludes. The tour is fascinating. We visit the King Center, and Dr. King's former home.

"I use to drive Dr. King around like this." The kindly man says to me.

"Were you his driver?" I ask.

He affirms and names a number of years of driving for Dr. King.

Another year, I decided to bus the attendees on Tuesday to Ebenezer Baptist Church. The first service is to begin at 9:30 AM. I contract with a bus company to bring attendees across the city. Along with a staff member and Reverend Anthony Bailey, a native of the Bahamas and now a pastor in Canada, I arrive at 8:45 AM to make ready the incredible sanctuary. The Reverend Raphael Warnock is scheduled to preach first and greets us as we enter the sanctuary. "David, I am ready to preach, but my choir director quit yesterday." This is frightening news because the choir director promised to design the liturgy for the service, and he promised to have an organist and special music. Anxiety sweeps me from toe to head. I know Anthony is a talented and gifted pastor. I turn to him, "Anthony can you lead this service?" Through his wonderful smile, he sends the calming words, "Yes, of course." At 9:30 AM, Anthony leads the congregation of over 1800 pastors in chants and acapella singing before Reverend Warnock preaches.

The contract with the bus company calls for them to have the buses at the church by 3:15 PM. The program will conclude at 3:30 PM. A flawless plan, I think, to have the pastors back across the city before rush hour. My compulsive inner self suggests I go outside the front of the church at 3:20 PM to make sure the buses are there. I look and see nothing, not one bus. My eyes scan in all directions. Nothing. I call the bus company. Dispatcher promises to check on the buses and call me back. The second anxiety wave of the day swells over me. The dispatcher calls back and says he talked with the lead driver and the buses are there. "I'm standing in front of the church and there are no buses!" I insist.

Looking at my watch, I see it is 3:29 PM. A few pastors exit the sanctuary early and join me in scanning the horizon for buses. None cometh! I call the dispatcher back. Then I see a long line of buses coming around from the back of the church. They line up, doors open, and pastors start boarding. I go to the lead bus driver. "Man, I almost had a heart attack. Where were you?" The lead driver explains: "We parked around back. This is Dr. King's church, and it would be disrespectful to leave our buses parked in front of his church." Humbled I say, "Oh, I see."

The *Festival of Homiletics* almost washes away in 2010. We are scheduled to be in Nashville and have an exciting lineup of speakers and musicians. Two weeks before the festival my phone buzzes early on a Sunday morning. The pastor of the host church in Nashville says, "David, have you heard about the flood?" I admit I had not. So Frank fills me in: "Nashville's having a flood of biblical size, not since the days of Noah."

The Tennessee River reached a flood stage never seen before with down-town mostly underwater. Businesses and restaurants ruined. The church, fortunately, sits on a hill and not flooded. The city, however, so damaged that Frank says, "David, I don't know if we'll be able to have the festival this year."

Nashville has a flood of water, but I have an immediate and intense flood of jaw clenching, teeth grinding anxiety. I can't reschedule to an-other city on that date. Speakers flights are booked, lots of advertising and expenses pre-paid. It could be a financial disaster.

Fortunately, Frank calls back in a few days and says he thinks we can do it. Lots of restaurants remain closed and parts of downtown are inac-cessible. About seventeen-hundred pastors attend, and the restaurants that could open tell us we saved their businesses because no one else is downtown after the epic flood.

We send out an email to all the pastors planning to attend and tell them what to expect with the flooded downtown, and how drinking wa-ter is limited. The city system contaminated. They should bring as much bottled water as they can. A group of pastors is coming from Ohio. One of the pastors calls, "We have an idea. We are renting U-Haul trucks, fill-ing them with cases of bottled water, and sending them to Nashville. And they did all week long before the *Festival of Homiletics*. So much bottled water that Frank calls to say "Thanks so much. Enough. We don't have any place to store more bottled water."

Two afternoons set aside as workdays, pastors venture out into the city and help with the cleanup. It is something to behold. We have a con-cert planned for Wednesday evening at the church by the famous Aus-tralian, but living in Nashville, guitarist Tommy Emmanuel. We ask the *Festival of Homiletics* attendees not to come to the concert. They agree. We open up the concert to the Nashville community, sell tickets, and turn the concert into a benefit concert for the recovery efforts, raising a great amount of money.

At this conference and several others, a speaker calls me on stage. I receive a standing ovation from nearly two thousand pastors. The *Festival of Homiletics* is the largest preaching conference in the world. *The New York Times*, *Time* magazine, and others interview me. Apparently, I have a national reputation of being an expert on preaching, although that is not accurate. My gift is bringing together teachers of homiletics and pastors.

I never cease to be amazed at how excited pastors and others are about the *Festival of Homiletics*. Every year at the *Festival of Homiletics*, attendees approach me and tell me the festival means so very much to them. They explain how their ministries are so difficult, but the festival helps them "recharge" their batteries. They call it "a lifesaver." Ministry is a lonely and isolated occupation. Congregations can have unrealistic expectations of pastors. Pastors often become frustrated with the resistance and stubbornness of congregations. The *Festival of Homiletics* provides an atmosphere of affirmation and encouragement for clergy that is often much needed. One of the greatest fulfillments in my life is hearing from these deeply appreciative pastors. I experienced tidal wave after tidal wave of encouragement. Indeed, I felt my calling was confirmed, in spite of Pastor Leroy's curse. *Festival of Homiletics's* pastors give me a surprise inheritance of affirmation for my work and ministry.

My phone rings one day. On the other end of the line is a representative of Marble Collegiate Church in New York City. Their pastor, Norman Vincent Peale, died a few years earlier. After a couple of interim pastors, they are searching for a permanent pastor. The church official on the phone wants me to make a recommendation for a person to be their new pastor, which I did. I was dumbfounded they wanted my opinion. I receive a similar call from The American Church in Paris! What would Pastor Leroy think? Does it make any difference? Am I still condemned to Hell?

A Serpent and A Father's Best Blessing

"The things that we love tell us what we are."

THOMAS ACQUINAS

AFTER A THEOLOGY CLASS in seminary, I no longer take Pastor "Grim Condemner" Leroy seriously. His threats long-festering deep in my psyche are exorcised. I know he has no basis for his condemnation. From what I learn about his life, he is the one who should worry about his mortal soul. Not too long after the "blue baptism," the church treasurer, who was treasurer for many years, dies. The new treasurer discovers Pastor Leroy received thousands of dollars each year for "ministerial expenses" and never turned in receipts. The now-deceased treasurer was apparently so intimidated by Pastor Leroy that he never questioned the practice. Additionally, there are rumors and eventually accusations of Pastor Leroy and sexual harassment.

Pastor Leroy knows he's losing popularity and support from his church. In desperation, he reverts to old mountain church practices and preacher ploys in attempts to re-charm his congregation. Pastor Leroy initiates "foot washing" to win back the men of the church. Once a month during Sunday morning worship, the pews on each side are turned sideways, facing each other. Men sit on one side and women on the other. After hymns and prayers, men take off their shoes, and the women are required to wash the mens' feet. Several women leave the church in protest.

Pastor Leroy announces he has received a new message from the Lord. In the most remote valleys high in the mountains, uneducated preachers to this day use Mark 16:18 ("They shall take up serpents.") to justify snake-handling during church services. These are usually churches of Pentecostal faith. Some of these preachers are bitten, and some die when they refuse medical treatment. The most clever preachers know the secret to snake handling, and Leroy knows the trick. During a sermon, Leroy trying to win back his congregants with a demonstration of great faith reaches behind the pulpit and pulls out a "three and a half foot" rattlesnake. He coddles the snake and boastfully claims to an awed and frightened congregation that God has given him a new spiritual gift.

Pastor Leroy brings out the snake for several services in the coming weeks. His church packs with people to witness the snake handling. Children shriek, women tremble, and men's eyes grow big. Pastor Leroy is winning back his congregation, but then he makes a mistake. After a service is over, he is in a lengthy conversation with a church member on the front steps. He forgets to take the container with the snake stuffed inside back to his office.

Little four-year-old Jamie Renfro wanders away from his mother while she chats with her friends in the sanctuary. The mother does not notice Jamie is going into the pulpit area. "Mommy, here's the snake! Come look!"

"Oh my God!" Jamie's mother screams as she runs toward the pulpit.

The snake poses no danger to Little Jamie, as Pastor Leroy was not in danger. Other church members and Jamie's mama see the snake in a cooler on ice underneath the pulpit. Snakes are cold-blooded. The ice puts them in a near dormant state, called brumation. The chilled snakes don't have the energy to bite. Pastor Leroy is bitten by shame. He does not wait to be fired. He packs his car that afternoon assumingly headed back to Transylvania County, North Carolina.

A rumor circulated in a few years that Pastor Leroy surfaced in San Diego, CA, as a member of Heaven's Gate, the cult of cults and a UFO-based religious group. According to the rumor, he escaped before thirty-nine bodies were discovered, the result of mass, ritual suicides.

Pastor Leroy's Hell was his own internal conflict of rigid beliefs projected upon the people he wanted to control. In the end, it all came crashing down upon him and must have felt like a Hell on earth at least for a few days.

What of the Howells? Doomed still? What of the Howell in the womb? The tortured fetus caught up in the cosmic struggle between the forces of Heaven and Hell? Did a professional ministerial career make up for the desperate hunger for acceptance, the hedonism of adolescence, and the random searching for life's meaning?

Is it enough simply to trust in the goodness and love of God? Do I hear "Tis" Murphy say? "Tis!" And is it true as Wendell Berry says, "There are no unsacred places; there are only sacred places and desecrated places."?

As I write this, Covid Virus rages all around. Sooner or later, due to Covid or "natural causes," friends and family will surround a hole in the ground, throw dirt in my face, and gather in a church fellowship hall to eat ham biscuits and brownies in my memory. Still, I don't fear death nearly as much as before. I wouldn't complain if an exception is made in my case of course. I don't like pain, so I think a quick death might be a gift as long as I get to say the appropriate goodbyes. Ahead at some point though looms a beautiful mystery.

What if my father pulling me away from the altar of instant salvation in Born Again Church in August of 1951 was a gift? I wandered to and fro on the face of the earth, but the journey, the search for theological clarity and meaning, continues wonderfully. Before their deaths, I wrote to my father and mother thanking them for the opportunities afforded me, gifts of good values, and especially the gift of an open mind.

My faith's curiosity might be unborn had my father not rescued me from the clutches of Pastor Leroy. A radical blessing for this hopeful universalist, a blessing as sweet as the summer rain falling from the Heavens that 1951 evening in Boonford.

". . . you single-handedly devised the *Festival of Homiletics*. What a major piece of work that will stand when the history of the U.S. church is written. It must be providential that you were led from your start to that great work that continues even now . . ." Walter Brueggemann[10]

Maybe as Barbara Brown Taylor said, I have indeed lived a charmed life!

Epilogue

PRESENTLY, I CONSULT WITH Luther Seminary, St Paul, MN, as they own and manage the festival. With Professor Karoline Lewis, I recruit speakers for the *Festival of Homiletics*. I recruited and introduced two sitting U.S. Senators at an event recently. Along with colleagues Karoline Lewis and Dawn Alitz, I secured the speakers for a pastors' conference on climate change with over 15,000 people from around the globe viewing virtually.

My mother is proud. I made it to "a piece of flat land" and "a warm house" as I live a quiet life on the shores of the Chesapeake Bay eating lots of seafood with a mountain-top retreat in Wintergreen, Virginia where I do field work as a Virginia Master Naturalist.

Endnotes

1. Minghella, *Cold Mountain.*
2. Hill, *Butch Cassidy and the Sundance Kid.*
3. Johnson, "Automobile."
4. Yang, "New Documentary."
5. Haines, "Tragic Ends."
6. Boschult, "'They would arrest anyone.'"
7. Sausser, "In SC, pregnant girls as young as 12 can marry."
8. Coen and Coen, *Oh Brother Where Art Thou?*
9. Brueggemann, *Festival of Homiletics* lecture, May 2011.
10. Brueggemann, email correspondence with the author, January 10, 2021.

Acknowlgements

PARENTS, BROTHER, AND SISTER for their patience with this troubled soul.

Flora Belle Robinson Roberson, neighbor, educator, and Christian community leader. Although I was not interested at the time, I saw her example as a thoughtful Christian, and I never forgot it.

Barbara Bailey, lay leader Wyliesburg Presbyterian Church, VA, gave me my first opportunity to teach a Bible class.

Teachers, mentors, supervisors, and therapists: William Lordi, Vic Maloy, Melvin Dowdy, Doris "Dodie" Rossell.

Understanding congregations who overlooked the mistakes of a zealous young pastor.

Writers for *Lectionary Homiletics* and the speakers for the *Festival of Homiletics*.

Lois, Denise, Beth, Sue, and others who made sure *Lectionary Homiletics* and events happened on schedule. (*Lectionary Homiletics* is available on *Atlas* in seminary libraries.)

Luther Seminary's Dawn Alitz and Karoline Lewis for giving me meaningful work to do.

Luther Seminary for their wonderful management of the *Festival of Homiletics*.

(I owe so many people, too many to list them all!)

Bibliography

Boschult, Christian. "'They Would Arrest Anyone': A Look Back at the Ocean Drive Jail and Easter Riot of 1967." *www.myhorrynews.com*.

Brueggemann, Walter. *Festival of Homiletics* lecture, May 2011.

Coen, Ethan, and Joel Coen, dirs. *Oh Brother Where Art Thou?* Buena Vista Pictures Distribution, December 22, 2000.

Haines, Don. "Tragic Ends: Frankie and Charlie Silver." www.blueridgecountry.com.

Hill, George Roy, dir. *Butch Cassidy and the Sundance Kid*. Twentieth Century Fox. Release date: September 23, 1969.

Johnson, Erik. "Collectible Classic: 1973–74 Volkwagon Thing." *Automobile*, www.automobilemag.com.

Minghella, Anthony, dir. *Cold Mountain*. Miramax Films. Release date: December 25, 2003.

Sausser, Lauren. "In SC, Pregnant Girls as Young as 12 Can Marry. There've Been 7,000 Child Brides in 20 Years." www.postcourier.com.

Yang, John. "New Documentary Presents Toni Morrison in Her Own Words." *PBS News Hour*. www.pbs.org.

000817542108192

9 781666 703962